International
Library of the
Philosophy of
Education

Experience
and the growth
of understanding

International Library of the Philosophy of Education

General Editor

R. S. Peters
Professor of Philosophy of Education
Institute of Education
University of London

Experience and the growth of understanding

D. W. Hamlyn

Professor of Philosophy
Birkbeck College
University of London

Routledge & Kegan Paul

London, Boston and Henley

First published in 1978
by Routledge & Kegan Paul Ltd
39 Store Street,
London WC1E 7DD,
Broadway House,
Newtown Road,
Henley-on-Thames,
Oxon RG9 1EN and
9 Park Street,
Boston, Mass. 02108, USA
Reprinted and first published
as a paperback in 1979
Set in 10 on 11 pt Baskerville by
Computacomp (UK) Ltd, Fort William
and printed in Great Britain by
Redwood Burn Ltd
Trowbridge and Esher

British Library Cataloguing in Publication Data

Hamlyn, David Walter

  Experience and the growth of
  understanding. – (International library of the
  philosophy of education).
  1. Children – Language 2. Cognition
  (Child psychology) 3. Child development
  I. Title II. Series
  401'.9   LB1139.L3   77–30215

  ISBN 0 7100 8735 7 (c)
  ISBN 0 7100 0336 6 (p)

To the memory of Theodore Mischel

Contents

General editor's note

There is a growing interest in philosophy of education amongst students of philosophy as well as amongst those who are more specifically and practically concerned with educational problems. Philosophers, of course, from the time of Plato onwards, have taken an interest in education and have dealt with education in the context of wider concerns about knowledge and the good life. But it is only quite recently in this country that philosophy of education has come to be conceived of as a specific branch of philosophy like the philosophy of science or political philosophy.

To call philosophy of education a specific branch of philosophy is not, however, to suggest that it is a distinct branch in the sense that it could exist apart from established branches of philosophy such as epistemology, ethics, and philosophy of mind. It would be more appropriate to conceive of it as drawing on established branches of philosophy and bringing them together in ways which are relevant to educational issues. In this respect the analogy with political philosophy would be a good one. Thus use can often be made of work that already exists in philosophy. In tackling, for instance, issues such as the rights of parents and children, punishment in schools, and the authority of the teacher, it is possible to draw on and develop work already done by philosophers on 'rights', 'punishment', and 'authority'. In other cases, however, no systematic work exists in the relevant branches of philosophy—e.g. on concepts such as 'education', 'teaching', 'learning', 'indoctrination'. So philosophers of education have had to break new ground—in these cases in the philosophy of mind. Work on educational issues can also bring to life and throw new light on long-standing problems in philosophy. Concentration, for instance, on the particular predicament of children can throw new light on problems of punishment and responsibility. G. E. Moore's old worries about what sorts of things are good in themselves can be brought to life by urgent questions about the justification of the curriculum in schools.

There is a danger in philosophy of education, as in any other applied field, of polarisation to one of two extremes. The work could be practically relevant but philosophically feeble; or it could be philosophically sophisticated but remote from practical problems. The aim of the International Library of the Philosophy of Education is to build up a body of fundamental work in this area which is both practically relevant and philosophically competent. For unless it achieves both types of objective it will fail to satisfy those for whom it is intended and fall short of the conception of philosophy of education which the International Library is meant to embody.

Professor Hamlyn's contribution to the Library is a brilliantly conceived and executed example of the fusion between the abstract and the concrete. His problem is the familiar one of how children acquire language and the part that language and experience play in this. He examines first of all the hoary empiricist thesis of genesis without structure; the opposing thesis, represented by Chomsky, of structure without genesis, is more kindly, but no less tellingly, criticised. And so he passes to Piaget, with whom he has most sympathy, who represents structure with genesis. However, Piaget's account is flawed by its biological model and by its failure to deal adequately with the problem of objectivity. So, having paid his respects to Piaget, Hamlyn, in the second part of the book, embarks upon his own account of these very difficult matters. It is an account in which a great deal more weight is placed than in the work of most philosophers on a child's pre-linguistic social experience in the genesis of understanding. His concern is to show how this and subsequent growth of understanding is possible.

This book should be compulsory reading for all serious students of child development and education; for nowhere else will they find these issues concerning Skinner, Chomsky and Piaget discussed with such rigour and clarity. It should also be of great interest to any philosophers who are concerned, as Locke was, with the genesis of knowledge and not just with the logical properties of its final outcome.

R. S. P.

Preface

While I have been interested in problems connected with learning for most of my philosophical life, I first became seriously involved in the problems put forward in this book some years ago when I was asked by Richard Peters to give a lecture on the subject at the Institute of Education in the University of London. At the time he and Paul Hirst went so far as to produce for me a list of questions which they wanted me to try to answer. The result was my 'The logical and psychological aspects of learning', which eventually appeared in *The Concept of Education* (ed. R. S. Peters). This was later followed by my first participation in the series of conferences of philosophers and psychologists organised by Theodore Mischel, from which there emerged on this occasion the book edited by him *Cognitive Development and Epistemology*. I am greatly indebted to these three persons for the stimulus that they gave me to follow out this line of thought. A final step in the process was my contribution on 'Human Learning' to the Royal Institute of Philosophy's conference on the Philosophy of Psychology which took place at Canterbury in 1971, at which my fellow-symposiast was John Morton of Cambridge and the chairman Theodore Mischel; the occasion was a most useful one for my purposes, and I am grateful to my fellow-participants and all those who made comments. The paper which I gave there eventually appeared in *The Philosophy of Psychology* (ed. S. C. Brown) and was reprinted in *The Philosophy of Education* (ed. R. S. Peters).

Parts of this book have been presented as papers or lectures in varying forms to audiences in various places both in Britain and in the USA and Canada. I am grateful to all those who have criticised and commented on my argument on those occasions, particularly perhaps Dr E. C. Olsen of OISE, Toronto, who has also read a draft of the book and made some helpful suggestions. I also read a preliminary draft of the book to a seminar at Birkbeck College during the summer term of 1974, and I am indebted to a number of people who attended the seminar and commented on sections of the book, particularly to my colleague at Birkbeck College, David Murray, and to Stephen Williams, who made specially pertinent criticisms.

My wife, Eileen, has read the typescript and made many useful comments. Her help, both in these ways and others, has been invaluable.

I am also grateful to my secretary, Miss Patricia Dymond, for assistance in all sorts of ways.

Introduction 1

A child is born into the world. At this point of time, when the child is just born, some would say that it is in effect simply an animal. It has undoubtedly something, indeed a great deal, of a human shape, and it possesses the physiological and other bodily equipment that will eventually make possible the performance of characteristic human functions, many of which will constitute distinguishing marks from the merely animal. (What those distinguishing marks are and whether there is anything that constitutes a clear and definite dividing line between the human and the animal is a question which I shall not discuss at this point. It has often been said that man possesses reason and animals do not, that man can use language and animals cannot, even that man has a soul and animals have not. I think that most of these claims for a sharp distinction become eroded after close examination and investigation. None of this, however, prevents it being the case that there are characteristic human functions and qualities, whether or not these are in any sense absolute.) A new-born child is even capable of certain forms of expression that one does not find in all animals, e.g. crying, though not as yet perhaps smiling or similar expressions of pleasure. Hence, to say that at this time the child is in effect simply an animal is to put a great deal of weight on the words 'in effect'. Indeed a new-born child lacks many of the functions and capacities of a grown animal, even a fairly lowly one; its sense-organs, for example, are very undeveloped and have at the best limited use. It would be fairer to say that a child is at this stage a living organism of a recognisably animal kind, but one which has not developed many of the functional capacities that animals in general come to possess, and even less of what we regard as characteristically human. Yet the child is equally and obviously a little human being; all being well, it will become what we fully recognise as such.

The process of development is also not typically animal. There are many capacities that adult animals possess and functions that they perform that a human child will not possess until some considerable time after animals born at the same time possess them. Walking and other means of locomotion will not come for some time; the same is true of self-nourishment. The same applies even to the use of the sense-organs; many animals born at the same time will see things in some way long before the young human will. All these are well-known facts that even an arm-chair philosopher can assert without much fear of contradiction. It is equally obvious that in the long run the human child will acquire capacities, skills, understanding and knowledge, as well as many other traits, far beyond anything that an animal can attain. In animals too, as the ethologists have pointed out, much often depends on what happens at crucial stages of development: unless a chick pecks at its mother's bill at a certain stage of its life it may never come to peck at all, and may therefore starve if not fed in other ways. This phenomenon, called by the ethologists 'imprinting', indicates how much may turn on the satisfaction of certain causal conditions at crucial stages of growth. It is not clear that this happens so much or so obviously in humans.[1]

Presumably a human child is in some sense conscious; but so are animals conscious in some sense, and all depends on the sense in question. Many years later the human child will, all being well, be conscious in ways that animals can never be. He or she will have forms of understanding that an animal could never have. That too is not a matter for dispute, nor presumably is the claim that the difference is founded on differences between human and ordinary animal physiology, though whether it is founded *solely* on these depends on certain aspects of the mind-body problem into which it would not be to the point to enter here.

So far, just as the facts seem unproblematic as facts, so there seems nothing problematic on the philosophical level, and one might wonder what a philosopher would be doing straying into this territory. Apart from my reference to the mind-body problem, the points that I have mentioned all seem to turn on matters of fact and there seems no problem which could be settled *a priori* or by arm-chair means. Yet there are philosophical problems in this area all the same. One might put the issues, or some of them, as follows. It appears that when a child is born it knows nothing and understands nothing—and I speak in a qualified way, speaking of what appears to be the case, only so as not to beg questions which will arise later. Years after birth (and how many years does not matter here) the human being who was a new-born child will have complex and extended knowledge and complex and involved forms of understanding. How does he or she acquire these? But why is this not a straightforwardly factual question which can be left to the psychologists and perhaps also to the sociologists? It cannot be denied that there are factual issues at stake here, but there is also the question of how we are to understand the process of the acquisition of knowledge and understanding. This will involve further questions about how we are to understand the concepts in terms of which learning (as I shall now call it without wishing to beg at this stage the question whether all learning involves the acquisition of knowledge) is to be seen and itself understood. It might be objected that these questions are still questions which arise within the theoretical framework of psychology and are thus not specifically philosophical. I think that this would be to take too narrow a view of what is philosophical.

Questions such as whether all knowledge is acquired from experience or whether there is any knowledge which is not so acquired have often been asked by philosophers in the past. It has sometimes been said, particularly by recent philosophers, that these are misleading ways of putting the proper philosophical questions. John Locke raised the question whether all our ideas come from experience and also whether all our knowledge comes from the same source; and he answered that all our ideas come from experience but, more equivocally, that all our knowledge does not so come. Kant maintained that all our knowledge comes through but not necessarily from experience. The philosophically tough-minded[2] have said that the question of the genesis of our ideas, for example, is a matter for psychology, the proper philosophical questions being about the logical character of different ideas and their application to the world. For this reason many philosophers in recent times have tried to avoid stating the questions which they take to be their proper concern in the way that Locke and others did in the seventeenth and eighteenth centuries, not to speak of others since. It is however surely the case that what we take ideas or concepts to be and what we take knowledge and its various forms to be must inevitably colour our conception of the ways in which these things can be said to be acquired, let alone how they are actually acquired. It is a matter of fact, as I shall try to show later, that epistemological theories have influenced the way in which learning has been construed by those professionally concerned with the phenomena of learning. One might respond to this by saying that this shows only that this is another area in which psychologists have had to struggle free from the influences of philosophers, and that they should continue so to struggle; in the process philosophy will be 'kicked upstairs' (as Austin thought would and should happen with the philosophy of language).

Such a conception feeds off the idea that philosophy exists only where the corresponding sciences are still merely embryonic. I do not think that this is true. The function of philosophy is not to put the sciences on the right path and then retire; such a view would be at once presumptuous and too modest. The fact is that in the area of learning many concepts get application that philosophers have had much to do with. Given that a concept has applicability in a certain area the question whether it should have application is one the answer to which depends on the facts, and for this reason it would be a rash philosopher who attempted to lay down the law on the application of those concepts without some knowledge, and preferably a considerable knowledge, of the facts. But I said 'given that a concept has applicability', and the question whether it has this might well be a question on which a philosopher could have something to say. The question is not off-limits to one who is professionally simply a philosopher. In any case, in areas such as the one under consideration the concepts involved are not particularly technical ones, and the concepts of knowledge and of a concept have been very much the concern of philosophers in one way or another, whatever be the questions with which they were properly concerned. Hence it might justly be supposed that philosophers could conceivably cast light upon the interconnection between such concepts and hence upon what learning involves. For *that* is a conceptual issue, an issue about how we are to understand that concept and the relations in which it stands to other concepts, such as those of knowledge, understanding and experience.

The question of how knowledge is related to experience is undoubtedly a philosophical question. So in a similar way must be the question of how we are to understand the way in which knowledge arises out of experience. It is indeed a philosophical question which ideally ought to be answered before attempts are made to sort out the circumstances in which learning is best carried on, and so forth. The last is undoubtedly a psychological issue, and there are many other psychological questions to be answered about the way in which individuals learn or perhaps about how people of certain general kinds learn and under what conditions. But these questions presuppose an answer to the question of what learning is, and this is a philosophical question whatever is the professional occupation of the person who asks or answers it.

Something of one of the major points at issue can be brought out by considering a passage from Plato's *Meno*, a passage which itself purports to say something about learning. At *Meno* 80d Meno himself raises the question of how one can carry on the business of an inquiry the end of which is knowledge. One might put the question by asking how one can learn something when what is to be learnt is an item of knowledge. Plato himself expresses the issue in terms of knowledge. What I have said so far does not make clear what is at stake. Meno's problem is expressed in the form of a dilemma: that either one knows already what one is trying to learn, in which case there is no need for the attempt; or one does not, in which case one will not know when one has succeeded in the attempt. Either one has the knowledge that one is trying to acquire or one has not; in the first case there is no need to acquire it (indeed one cannot strictly speaking *acquire* it), while in the second case one will not be in the position to recognise the goal when one is there. The dilemma is presented as a sophistical one and has often been characterised by others as mere sophistry; for clearly we do carry on inquiries, sometimes with success, and we do learn things. What plausibility the dilemma has seems to depend on the idea that we either have something before the mind or we do not; and this second dilemma seems obviously invalid. We can know some things about our goal without, so to speak, knowing *it*, and our knowledge of the specification of the goal to be attained may enable us to recognise whatever answers to the specification in question. It may be that Plato was limited or was limiting himself in his conception of knowledge to the idea that knowledge is simply a direct awareness of the thing in question.

However that may be, there is another point to be abstracted from the discussion, and this is one that emerges in part from Plato's own 'solution'. This 'solution' is not one that would appeal to us today. He says that the soul has been through many lives and in doing so has seen all things, although it has forgotten them. It needs only to be reminded of them, however, by being confronted with them in its present existence. Plato offers to demonstrate the truth of the doctrine by getting a boy to 'recollect' the solution to a geometrical problem without actually informing him of the answer or positively teaching him what it is. We need not here go into the problem in question in any detail. It is in fact the problem of the length of the side of a square which is twice the area of a given square. Socrates is made to ask the boy questions which are in fact leading questions, and even adds to the initial geometrical figure constructions which enable the boy to see the correct solution. At the end it is said that the boy is in a dream-like state which is in fact not knowledge, but merely true belief; this can however be converted into knowledge by repeated and varied questions. In one way the example is a cheat, because what the boy has to do is to work out the consequences of things that he does already know and understand, as is normal in working through a geometrical proof, even if he has to be made to approach the problem from a new direction or with a new slant. Not all learning is like that. Nevertheless Plato claims that the 'demonstration' shows that the boy really knew the solution all along and needed only to be reminded of it; so all learning is recollection. I said that not all learning is like that, but it is of course true that Plato could not have 'demonstrated' his thesis in that way in cases of learning where what has to be learnt is an empirical truth, not an *a priori* one, as a geometrical truth must be. That is what I meant when I said that what the boy has to do is to work out the logical consequences of what he already knows, even if he has to be jogged along in the process. The 'demonstration' is therefore something of a fraud and it cannot be taken as showing that all learning is recollection. It is important, however, that it is because he has relevant knowledge already that the boy is able to go through the learning process that he does go through.

Its importance is obvious enough in the kind of case in question, where the boy has to put together pieces of knowledge that he already has and abstract their consequences. But it is important for other kinds of learning too. One might put the point by asking how it is possible to use experience in learning if one does not know something about what in that experience is relevant to the task. The successful use of any tool presupposes a knowledge about the applicability of the tool to the task in hand. Many inquiries are such that experience has to be used as a tool for the solution of the problem which is the inquirer's concern. It might be objected, however, that it is not always like that. Even in those forms of learning which involve the acquisition of knowledge in a direct way, that acquisition of knowledge does not always come as the result of an inquiry. Hence it may not always be appropriate to speak of the *use* of experience. That, however, does not affect the general point. Even when a person is given a piece of information he will not thereby acquire knowledge unless that 'information' has an intelligibility for him; and for that to be the case it has to fit in with what he knows in some way or other. Otherwise it will not function as information proper. New knowledge thus builds on old knowledge. Where the Platonic example is misleading is not in its display of that fact, but in its suggestion that the way in which the building is carried on is always like that involved in solving a geometrical problem. For in the example in question the 'building' involves the application of knowledge about what squares and things of that kind are, in such a way as to make it possible for the inquirer to see what is implied in that knowledge as far as concerns a particular case. For that is the nature of the knowledge acquired: it is an implication of the knowledge with which he starts, and given it he is capable in principle (although not necessarily in fact) of working out the conclusion from what he already knows without further experience. That is what is implied in saying that the knowledge so acquired is *a priori*.

But where a person has to acquire through experience knowledge of new facts (or facts that are new to him at least) it is not like that at all. He cannot in that case apply the knowledge that he already has by simply working out its implications or consequences; or rather he cannot do this alone. The experience has to provide him with genuinely new information. But my point is that experience cannot do this unless it is somehow fitted into an already existing web of understanding and knowledge, unless, that is, the experience is significant for the learner. But the 'fitting in' will not always be a matter of seeing that the information derived from experience follows from the previously existing knowledge. If I notice that the house down the road has just been painted a new colour (say, blue) I shall have learnt a new fact, which may, so to speak, simply be set alongside other pieces of knowledge that I may have, and which need not have any particular implications for anything else. Let alone be implied by anything else that I know. Yet this could not have been a new fact for me if I did not know what it was for something to be blue, or perhaps if I did not know what paint was and what it was for something to be painted. So while the new knowledge is not implied by those items of knowledge it does presuppose them in some way. Seen in this way the growth of knowledge must inevitably appear as a structure becoming ever more complicated, within which there are extremely complex relationships, eventually too complex to unravel. One question that may be raised nevertheless is whether there is any necessity that the structure should conform to any general principles, so that while one may not be able to plot its details one may be able to determine the general laws that govern it. A further question that would arise if the answer to the first question is 'Yes' is: what is the nature of that necessity?

Piaget thinks that it is indeed possible to lay down certain principles which govern cognitive development, so that one can say that there is a definite development of knowledge and experience, and one can distinguish definite stages through which the individual must pass in it. I shall give some consideration to what he has to say about this in a later chapter, and I shall equally try to say something about the second question that I have mentioned: what is the nature of the necessity according to which an individual must necessarily pass through these stages. Piaget also indicates two rival positions to which he is opposed in all this. They are, roughly, empiricism and rationalism respectively, although he does not always use those titles. He calls them geneticism without structure and structure without genesis. The point of these terms is that empiricism, as Piaget sees the general tendency of that movement (and it is not an entirely inaccurate description), involves the idea that knowledge and understanding develop or grow in the individual without the growth conforming to any general principles; they come about and grow adventitiously, as experience comes, where it happens to fall, so to speak. Hence there can be no principles that govern their growth. The opposing idea, which rationalism tends to embrace, is that the individual is born with the principles of his subsequent intellectual development already built in. Hence there is a sense in which, according to this view, there is no new development. What we may *call* that is in fact prefigured in the structure with which the individual is equipped when born. (The biological parallel is the doctrine of preformation, according to which the subsequent growth of the organism is laid down in the germ-plasm, and this is an idea that Piaget equally repudiates; he uses the notion of 'prefiguration' but not in that way.)

If all learning was of the form that Plato considers in the 'geometrical example', it would mean that all new knowledge is merely an implication of what we are born with. It would thus involve structure without genesis in the sense that Piaget has in mind. Experience would figure only as the means by which the working out of the implications of inborn structures is touched off. Plato himself says that experience reminds us of what we already know, so that strictly speaking there is not on his view any real acquisition of new knowledge. Such a view provides what is almost a paradigm of structure without genesis; and other views to be found in the writings of rationalist thinkers provide parallels to a greater or less extent. Indeed it has often been said that Plato's theory is his 'substitute' for a theory of innate ideas or knowledge, such as is found in some rationalists. The only reason for qualification in speaking of a 'substitute' is that Plato supposes that the knowledge has in fact been acquired through experience of some kind in a previous life. The snag with this is that, whatever one may think of the possibility of previous lives, the previous acquisition of knowledge ought to be construable on the lines of how knowledge is acquired in this life. That is to say that it too ought to be a matter of being reminded of what one previously knew. Such a view clearly generates an infinite regress which is vicious since there can be no first acquisition of knowledge; for that reason the view is incoherent. The same objection does not apply to the view that we are simply born with knowledge, although there are other objections to this that will emerge later.

The view that Piaget labels 'geneticism (or genesis) without structure'—empiricism in a radical sense—presents its own problems. For one thing, if knowledge comes about in the individual just as experience falls, it would be at best just a happy chance if it were to result in anything common to different individuals. Agreement would be a matter of coincidence, given the extent to which experience varies from one person to another. It might be argued on the other side that we do after all inhabit a common world. Why then should it be surprising if individuals do acquire knowledge and understanding in a common way? It is in fact far from clear that this consideration is really compelling. There is certainly a sense in which we live in the same world, but it is a very complex world and people may be affected by it very differently. Under what conditions could it become to each of us in so many respects the *same* world? We are, in our upbringing, initiated into a common understanding, one which is in part culturally determined but also in part determined by general human sensibility and other features that human beings have in common. Wittgenstein has emphasised the important role that is played by what he calls 'forms of life' in which we all share, and which provide the foundation for 'agreement in judgments' without which in turn language could not get a purchase.[3] The same considerations apply to understanding in general. We cannot presume that just because we are all human beings and because many of us are born into a roughly similar environment it is enough to ensure a common and agreed understanding. It has indeed sometimes been claimed that just the opposite must obtain if the empiricist theory holds good. Thus Russell in his 'Lectures on the Philosophy of Logical Atomism'[4] claims that what one man understands by 'Piccadilly' must necessarily differ from what another man understands by it, just because their experiences of it must necessarily differ. So they must, unless we presume in them a common understanding, prior to experience, of what Piccadilly is. But it is just this that we cannot presume if it is true that understanding and knowledge come about just as experience comes or falls. In other words, a strict empiricist is committed to the consequence that agreement in understanding, without which knowledge as we comprehend it must be impossible, must be coincidental and a happy chance at best.

Piaget attempts to steer a middle course between the two extreme positions to which he is opposed. He wants, that is, genesis *with* structure. If that is to be the case there must be principles that govern the growth of knowledge and understanding in the individual, principles which are a function of the system constituted by the individual and his environment. It has sometimes been said that Piaget presents an account of human learning without a theory of learning. In a sense that is true. His theory is one of the so-called cognitive development of the individual as a function of principles that govern the system which the individual plus his environment comprise. The result is a kind of Kantianism. For Kant the understanding in application to experience must, if that experience is to be objective, conform to certain *a priori* principles. For Piaget the development of understanding in relation to experience must, if it is to lead to mature and objective experience and understanding, conform to principles that govern the course of that development. Thus on this account there is not a sheer contingency about the growth of understanding, and for that reason not a sheer contingency about the growth of knowledge in the individual either. Yet this kind of theory cannot explain the community of knowledge and understanding, any more than the opposing theories can. For they all start from the same starting-point—the individual set over against his environment—so that the way in which 'cognitive development' takes place must be a function of these two variables and of the relations that exist between them. (I put these words in quotation marks because I have scruples about too light an acceptance of the notion of development in this context. See my paper, 'The Concept of Development', *Proceedings of the Philosophy of Education Society of Great Britain*, (1975). It is difficult, however, to avoid the term altogether in these contexts, and I shall not always try to do so in the following.)

It must be explained how agreement between individuals, something which, if Wittgenstein is right, stands at the foundations of knowledge, can come about. None of the theories so far reviewed really explains this, since on these theories other people exist for the individual simply as part of the individual's environment, as objects, and not, as we might put it, co-subjects.

These issues (to which I shall return in more detail in succeeding chapters) bring to the fore, therefore, a number of problems which may be brought together by asking how and what makes it possible that an individual born into the world in the way that I have indicated, with his individual potentialities and capacities, can develop an understanding and knowledge which is both objective and shared with others. A second problem which has to be fitted in with this is how, if it is really true that the acquisition of knowledge through learning presupposes knowledge in one way or another, the business ever gets going at all. For does not the dependence of knowledge on knowledge generate a regress which can be stopped only by supposing that one is born with knowledge in the first place? Or must one relax the principle in question, and if so, how? It must be remembered that the reason for invoking the principle was that without it there would be no way in which the relevance and intelligibility of any given item in experience could be evident to the individual. It should be clear that this way of regarding the matter presupposes a degree of sophistication on the part of that individual. Its relevance to the adult learner needs little justification; but in the case of an infant the situation seems different. It would scarcely seem reasonable to regard the infant as trying to make sense of his experiences as a way of coming to understand the world into which he has come to exist. It is tempting to regard the child as an adult writ small, but the temptation should be resisted. For one thing, the child is not like a little scientist putting questions to nature and attempting to elicit answers; such a view would make no sense although it has sometimes been espoused in one form or other.[5] Hence we must look for a different approach. One thing that is extremely important about the infant's finding his way in the world is that he has to be put in the way of things by adults; his attention is thus directed and focused, in such a way that questions of relevance would not need to arise even if they could. For this reason the factors that are important in an adult inquirer or even in an adult getting information in a more passive way need not have the same importance in the infant.

Another vital point is that the child is not a solitary centre of consciousness who has to make sense of its world by his or herself. He or she stands in relations to other human beings almost from the beginning, and it is very important in this that the child is treated as a person. Hence social considerations arise from the very beginning of life. Parents do not behave towards the child exactly as teachers, but there is much in their behaviour towards the child that is in a genuine sense educational. In this particular educational context the part played by attitudes which one might describe as emotional, attitudes such as love, is extremely important. If motivational and emotive factors play a part throughout the whole of learning, they are all-important at the beginning. I shall have more to say about this later. It is in this area that I think we must look for a solution to the problem of how the growth of knowledge and understanding gets going.

One final point by way of introduction: I have spoken in the foregoing on several occasions of 'understanding or knowledge'. This may be misleading if it is taken to imply that there is no real difference between the two. When I have put the two together so far I have done so because it seemed to me that nothing turned on the distinction in the contexts in question. It is clear that knowledge of facts presupposes understanding of the ideas in terms of which the facts are to be expressed or formulated; but knowledge of facts is not quite the same as understanding those same facts, and I do not mean to suggest otherwise. Equally, understanding a person, for example, is not quite the same as knowing him, or at any rate it need not be. It may be that I cannot really know a person without understanding him, but there are lesser forms of knowledge of persons which do not necessarily imply understanding to the same extent. Yet such considerations are not quite to the point in the immediate context. For when we speak of the growth of understanding this might just as easily be expressed in terms of the growth of knowledge. To understand a thing or a situation (if not a person) is surely to know what it is for something to be a thing of the kind in question, what it is for that situation to hold good. In other words, while knowledge of facts presupposes understanding in the way indicated earlier but without the knowledge being identical with that understanding, understanding something may itself be explicated in terms of a form of knowledge. Thus the growth of understanding is in effect the growth of one kind of knowledge. Hence in what follows the distinction will be maintained only where something turns on it.

Genesis without structure   2

I have referred to Plato as an example of a thinker who provides an account of the genesis of knowledge which is, if not explicitly rationalist in character, nevertheless a variation on that theme. Aristotle is, by contrast, often spoken of as an empiricist. If one has in mind in considering this assessment the issues of traditional epistemology it is not altogether clear that the judgment is a correct one. By 'issues of traditional epistemology' I mean the concern with such questions as whether all our knowledge is founded on experience. If this question is taken to be the question whether all propositions that express knowledge can be validated by reference to experience, it is not in fact a question about the genesis of knowledge, even if some philosophers (e.g., perhaps Locke) have seemed to want to tackle it by raising genetic questions. In Aristotle's case the situation is complicated by the fact that although there are some suggestions in his writings that all our ideas are dependent ultimately on sense-perception (or, as it came to be put, there is nothing in the intellect that was not previously in the senses),[1] his conception of knowledge itself raises more complex issues.

Aristotle frequently says that we have knowledge proper when we know the reason why. This knowledge proper, as I have called it, is *episteme*, scientific knowledge as Aristotle sees it. It is the knowledge that something must be so because it is derivable by demonstrative forms of argument from premises which must also be so. But if this process of reason-giving or justification is not to go on for ever—something which would undermine the claim to have knowledge proper—there must be ultimate first principles of such demonstration. Thus Aristotle believes that scientific knowledge depends ultimately on certain first principles from which the truths of each science are derived or derivable. These truths can therefore be demonstrated and thereby taught by showing that they follow from the first principles by strict, demonstrative rules, such as are involved in the demonstrative syllogism. It is Aristotle's belief that the subject-matter of each science can be displayed in this fashion. It follows from this that the reason for any truth so derived can be exhibited by reference to the middle term of the demonstrative syllogism (which is necessarily a syllogism in the first figure) through which the truth is demonstrated. Aristotle's view is in this respect not implausible. Thus in the syllogism 'All B is C, all A is B, so all A is C' (a so-called syllogism in 'Barbara'), the middle term B supplies the reason why all A is C. We might ask 'Why is it the case that all A is C?' and the answer might be 'Because of B; for all B is C and all A is B'. The *way* in which B constitutes the reason why the final truth holds good will depend on the nature of the truths involved.[2] This whole way of thinking, however, presupposes, as we have seen, that there are ultimate first principles with reference to which we cannot similarly ask the question 'Why?'. If knowledge of the derived truths comes through demonstration, how does the knowledge of the first principles themselves come about? Indeed, how can this properly be called knowledge if, as must be the case, it presupposes *no* knowledge of the reason why the first principles hold good? On this last point Aristotle attempts a solution by invoking other conceptions of knowledge than *episteme* itself. But he remains clear that whatever be the intellectual state that we have towards the first principles it must be more precise or definite than the knowledge of the truths derived from them; for the latter depends on the former and is teachable only through the former. How then does that knowledge, if knowledge it is, come about?

It is interesting for our purposes that Aristotle (*P.A.* II, 19) presents the problem in a way that is an obvious if oblique reference to the issue raised in Plato's *Meno*, an issue which he discusses more directly elsewhere in the *Posterior Analytics* (71a29). He asks whether the states of knowledge, or capacities involved in knowledge (*gnorizousai hexeis*), of the first principles are such that they come about without previously existing or are there all the time without our being aware of it. The dilemma is akin to, although not quite identical with, that put forward by Meno, and Aristotle finds fault with each horn of the dilemma. He says that it would be strange if we had the states of knowledge all the time; for in that case we should have knowledge more precise than that which is demonstrated, yet without our being aware of having it. (The implication is presumably that precision is a matter of having whatever it is clearly before the mind; Aristotle's slant upon the *Meno* dilemma presupposes a certain appreciation of what lies behind it, so that his way of presenting the issues is not quite the same as Plato's.) On the other hand, if we acquire the states of knowledge without having had them before how can we come to know and learn from a knowledge which has not previously existed? (Once again Aristotle seems to have grasped something of the underlying issues of the *Meno*, since the implication of his remark is that the acquisition of knowledge does indeed presuppose other knowledge.)[3] His resolution of the difficulty involves in part a piece of genetic epistemology, as Piaget calls it; it is a brief account of how knowledge is made possible by development from an inborn potentiality possessed by all animals, an 'inborn discriminative potentiality' or an 'inborn potentiality for judgment' which men call sense-perception. The account is far from being Piagetian, but it is recognisably a theory in the same area as that of Piaget.

The traditional account of Aristotle's argument is that it is aimed at showing how intuition of first principles comes about as the result of induction. The last, induction, is a way of coming to see general principles in particular cases and depends on the development of experience in the way that Aristotle indicates in his genetic account. I do not think that this is the right view of induction as Aristotle employs that notion.[4] Rather induction is a form of argument which a teacher may use to get someone to see the truth of a principle by reference to cases (and a man may of course be his own teacher). The genetic account is not a theory of induction but a theory of the development of potentialities that make the use of induction possible and fruitful. Each stage of the genetic account, on this view, merely presents a theory of what is necessary if the next stage is to be possible, but not a theory of what is sufficient for this purpose. (Similar comments are relevant to Piaget's views and I shall return to the point later.) In what follows I have tried to present Aristotle's views without too much dependence on this issue.

His theory is of a piece with his general view of how capacities develop; it fits, for example, what he says in the *Nicomachean Ethics* (at the beginning of Bk II) about moral virtues or capacities coming about by habituation: that we become good or just by doing good or just things, provided that this is supplemented by practical reason. Indeed the very terminology in which he sets out the issues and the resulting theory indicate the same thing. Aristotle believes that states or capacities (*hexeis*) come about in living things or at any rate in rational beings[5] through the exercise of potentialities (*dunameis*) that they naturally possess. The exercise of those potentialities requires a cause, but when it happens regularly in beings of this kind there is generally set up a *hexis* or capacity which, given a cause, may be manifested in activity (*energeia*). Exactly what are, in Aristotle's view, the criteria for something's counting as an activity in this sense has been much disputed by scholars, but it is at least true that an activity needs no further end outside itself. At all events the exercise of the *hexis* is related to the exercise of the initial potentiality or *dunamis* in the way that doing just things out of justice is related to doing things that simply happen to be just (without, so to speak, the intention or concern for justice). But the *hexis* itself is set up by mere habituation and is thus contingent upon the way in which experience falls. It is for this reason that the process can justly be described as genesis without structure.

The details of Aristotle's genetic account of what makes knowledge of first principles possible when supplemented by induction are as follows. In animals where this is possible there may result from sense-perception a persistence of the perception (the state or percept), which constitutes or gives rise to memory. From memory when this occurs many times with reference to the same thing there arises what Aristotle calls experience (*empeiria*, from which is derived the word 'empirical'). This is experience in roughly the sense in which we use the term when we speak of a man of experience or say 'My experience of this is ... '. It is an accumulated commonsense knowledge of things that comes about through perception. At the beginning of the *Metaphysics*, where Aristotle repeats much of what he says in our passage at the end of the *Posterior Analytics*, he adds that experience is concerned with particulars and is to be contrasted with scientific knowledge in this respect. One can see why he says this although, as he himself admits, it is not true that it has no concern with universals; one can experience things as such and suches or perceive the universal in the particular. Nevertheless experience is always connected with particular things and particular occasions and conditions. In the *Posterior Analytics* he goes on to say that from experience or 'from the universal fixed as a whole in the soul, a one over many, whatever is one and the same in them all, is the source of art and scientific knowledge—art if it is concerned with coming to be, scientific knowledge if it is concerned with what is'. The language in this passage, especially the reference to a one over many, is Platonic, but the universal referred to is an item of knowledge of a universal or general kind, something that is expressible in the form of an 'All A is B' proposition, given that the function of such a proposition is in this context to express what is essential to A. Aristotle goes on to elucidate his idea by means of an analogy with a rout stopped in battle, where, he says, one man stands firm, then another and another, until the company reforms as at the beginning. The analogy is perhaps not altogether perspicuous in detail, but the general idea is clear enough: the repetition of experiences of a similar kind leads to the setting up of a universal judgment. The resulting state of mind is called by Aristotle 'intuition', but this is brought about by induction, once given the development of potentialities along the lines of the genetic account. Induction itself is a case of getting someone to see the truth of the principles by making use of experience, which implies knowledge of *cases*.

An example given at the beginning of the *Metaphysics* might lead us, on the other hand, to think that by 'induction' Aristotle means what it has come to mean since: the surveying of instances in order to set up a generalisation. For he speaks of the judgment that a certain remedy was good for a disease in the case of Callias, Socrates, etc., leading to the judgment that it is good for all men of a similar constitution in similar circumstances. But Aristotelian induction is rather to be seen, as I have indicated, as the process of getting someone to see the universal principle in the instances. It has something in common with the use of induction by Socrates (indeed Aristotle says that Socrates was the first to use induction), and Socrates, to judge from the Platonic dialogues, seems to have *used* instances or examples to give point to a general principle rather than abstracting a principle from the instances. However this may be, induction presupposes the development of a potentiality for perceptual knowledge, and the suggestion is that this comes about by repetition within experience, just as moral virtue may be set up in a man by habituation. The process seems relatively, if not entirely, mechanical, especially if repetition at one stage is thought of as a sufficient condition for development of the next; although this may not be what Aristotle intended. A similar mechanical conception has been embraced by other thinkers in a broadly empiricist tradition, especially those belonging to the movement known as 'Associationism', which flourished in the nineteenth century and before. Indeed, such an idea can be found in a very clear form in the writings of David Hartley, particularly his *Observations on Man* (1749).

Yet it is far from clear, when one begins to think about it, how the process is supposed to work, although it gains some plausibility if the different stages are thought of merely as necessary conditions of the next. I shall, however, assume in what follows that more is intended than this by Aristotle, although this may not be the case. The final stage, the seeing of the general principle in the instances, has a certain intelligibility about it, to the extent that one can well accept that it occurs. We do sometimes come to see a general principle working in a number of particular cases. But this is hardly to be described as the fixing

17

of a universal in the soul as a result of repetition of experiences. If one comes to see a general principle as applying to instances it may be for various different reasons but it will rarely, if ever, be due to purely mechanical causes. That is to say that in explaining how it is that someone has come to see that a certain principle holds good it will rarely, if ever, be plausible to say that this has been brought about by mechanical or quasi-mechanical processes. We do sometimes say of someone that something caused him to see that a certain principle holds good; indeed this is the point of the popular and no doubt apocryphal story of Newton and the falling apple. But what we really imply by this way of talking is that this was the occasion for his coming to see the principle; we do not imply anything like causality in a mechanical sense.

Whatever be the truth about that, there are greater difficulties in the earlier stages of the process as they seem to be described by Aristotle. One of the points may be brought out by attention to a phrase which he uses in summing up after the analogy of the stopping of a rout. He speaks of one of the undifferentiated things standing firm. What in fact differentiates an item out of the undifferentiated things? We are given to understand that it is in effect simply the repetition of the item, or rather a repetition of items at different levels: first perception, then memory, then experience. But at each level the processes involved seem on this view of them merely mechanical, and this affects the question of how the concepts used in the account are to be understood. It seems that the repetition of sense-perceptions is construed rather as the repetition of sensations, which produces a sense-impression. This when repeated produces a memory-impression, and this in turn experience, and so on. But how does the repetition of sensations produce the persistent sense-impression, how does this in turn constitute memory, and how does the repetition of a memory bring about the seeing that a particular has a certain general characteristic? To put the matter in the context of Aristotle's remark about differentiation, what could make what is undifferentiated into something differentiated?

Repetition is surely not a sufficient explanation here. For by 'undifferentiated' Aristotle can only mean that the items in question are not initially differentiated by the person concerned. It is not that they are not differentiated or different in themselves. Otherwise there could not be different effects and no sense could be given to the idea of an item producing different effects. One can see why in certain circumstances a person might be got to differentiate an item from others through its being repeatedly

brought to his attention. Repetition might be one factor leading
to a person's differentiation of an item, although there might well
be other factors as well, such as the unusual character of the item
or its striking difference from its surroundings. But such
considerations bring out why a person might have his attention
drawn to a certain thing as distinct from others. They are not
relevant to the question of what causal processes are involved. To
think in terms of causal processes is to suppose that there are
already distinct things which could act as causes producing distinct
effects. But that is the very question at issue. The idea is
presumably that a child is confronted repeatedly with, say, men,
and that this stamps into his soul the 'picture' of a man, so that
what gets singled out in this way is what the child is confronted
with most often. But most often as opposed to what? When we
speak in this way we normally have in mind already a range of
differentiated or differentiable things, one of which can be singled
out from the others by its repetition in our experience. Hence we
might gain the particular item of knowledge 'This is a man, *as
opposed to that*', or possibly 'A man is this, *as opposed to that*'. But if this
is the level of knowledge that is being supposed to be acquired it is
clear that the acquisition of knowledge of this kind presupposes a
good deal of knowledge already. It presupposes knowledge of the
range of differentiable items and therefore knowledge of a range
of contrasts and similarities. Repetition in this context could serve
to draw our attention to some of these contrasts and similarities,
but it could not do so unless we had some prior awareness of the
sort of thing that they were in general. Hence, repetition of sense-
perceptions in the way contemplated in this account of Aristotle
could not be sufficient to form a basis for knowledge without
reference to anything else.

It might be argued by way of objection to what I have said that
what is wrong is not the principles involved in the Aristotelian
account, but the example in terms of which I have chosen to
discuss it. After all, knowledge of what it is for something to be a
man is presumably fairly complex knowledge, and it is thus not
surprising that it presupposes other knowledge. To use the
language of classical empiricism, the idea of a man is a complex
idea; for simple ideas we should have to look for other examples,
such as the idea of a particular colour, e.g., red. But the objections
to the account apply even here; they are in fact one variety of well-
known objections to the possibility of so-called ostensive
definitions, the idea that one can elucidate the meaning of certain
terms by direct reference to experience.[6] Knowledge that 'this is
red' involves knowledge that it is red as opposed to other colours,

and therefore presupposes knowledge of what it is for something to be a colour and for there to be differences between colours. Repetition of experience, therefore, might, given that background knowledge, bring about the realisation that a certain particular thing has a certain colour. Repetition of *kinds* of experience might bring about the realisation that things of a certain *kind* have that colour; and this would undoubtedly presuppose memory, though not necessarily as an event the repetition of which itself is an indispensable part of the process. But the key-term in this is 'realisation'; one cannot realise something without this involving the application of knowledge that one has already. Hence the Aristotelian account has perhaps an application, although a limited one, to the ways in which we sometimes realise that things are so and so as a result of the course of experience. Nevertheless, as I said earlier, there are clearly other factors that may play a part in this apart from the mere repetition of experience (and it is possible that Aristotle thought so too, even if he gives us no idea of what they are). But the account cannot function as a complete account of how knowledge and understanding come about in the first place.

Could one, however, modify the account in such a way as to preserve the principle that knowledge and understanding come about through repetition of experience? The idea that the human (and presumably animal) organism is really a classifying mechanism has seemed an attractive one to many. If one combines this idea with the one that the classification is a function of the frequency with which groups of stimuli fall together, and that the organism simply responds to whatever affects it with the greatest frequency, one has a framework of theory which underlies much of empiricist thinking about learning. One example of this approach is to be found in F. A. Hayek's *The Sensory Order* (discussed on pp. 97–102 of my *Psychology of Perception*); others are to be found among proponents of that strand of behaviourism that lays predominant weight on what E. L. Thorndike called the Law of Exercise, in which habit is all, particularly J. B. Watson, the founder of behaviourism. There is of course no *a priori* reason why the human or animal organism should constitute a system of this kind, one which is maximally plastic and the state of which is therefore a complete function of the frequency of the effects on it brought about by the environment. (Even Watson's behaviourism had to presuppose certain innate reactions or responses which could be modified in experience through mechanisms such as conditioning; it did not therefore suppose that the organism was completely plastic.)

Given what we know about physiology such a theory is not even very plausible, let alone to be accepted *a priori*, for we should expect responses or reactions to the environment to be affected to some extent or other by the structure of the nervous system.

Even if the theory were plausible, however, it would still be very difficult to see how one gets from it to an explanation of how one *knows* things. It is all very well when one confines oneself to reactions or responses, for in the present context this would mean little more than that the system is affected in some way by repetition of stimuli. If this were expressed in terms of how the person or animal sees things—and it is a very large step indeed to this—it would amount at best to the point that the person or animal in question is caused in this way to see the objects that function as or serve to produce stimuli as similar to each other and thereby different from other things. Hence on this view the growth of experience would amount to the building up of similarities and differences on the basis of the perception of bare and basic similarities and differences (a perception which would involve no awareness of the *respect* in which the things in question were similar or different). If such perception of similarities and differences were to be based on repetition of stimuli it could be so only in the sense that we see those similarities and differences with which we are confronted most frequently. In other words, we see things as similar or different to the extent that they produce similar or different effects in us, and it is presumed that they will have similar effects to the extent that they fall together with the greatest frequency. I cannot say that I find this last notion very intelligible. It involves the idea that similarity is ultimately reducible to frequency of occurrence, and in this respect the account is on a par with those accounts of the association of ideas that attempt to reduce association by similarity or contrast to association by contiguity.

One could, of course, jettison the suggestion that frequency or repetition plays a crucial part in the way that experience develops. To do so, however, would be to jettison the one principle which, on the empiricist view so far considered, governs the growth of experience. If the principle is not in itself very readily intelligible it is nevertheless a principle and the only one available. If one can put it in terms of the analogy which has often been invoked since Plato used it in the *Theaetetus*—that of the wax tablet which is empty at birth, Locke's *tabula rasa*—the growth of experience is a function of the frequency of indentations of a given kind on the wax, so that the mind is structured according to the predominant role given to the deepest and therefore most prominent indentations. As long as one does not inquire too closely into the model it has a certain attractiveness. Without the principle that I have mentioned there is no sense in speaking of a *development* in experience, since in that case a man must perceive similarities and differences, if he does, without any rule governing how he does so. It will not do to say that people see those similarities and differences that actually obtain. First, we do not in fact attend to all similarities and differences, and we need some explanation why we attend to some and not others. Second, and more importantly, we have not as yet given any proper sense to the idea of what actually obtains; we have not given any proper sense to the notion of objectivity in this context, and it is questionable whether the model can provide it.

Let us, however, consider frequency or repetition simply as a principle which governs the growth of experience and not also as an explanation of how we come to see similarities and differences at all. That is to say, let us consider it as the basic explanation, given that people are capable of seeing similarities and differences at all, of why they see those that they do; for that is perhaps what Aristotle intended. It is supposed then that we come to be able to recognise general principles because of the repetition of experience and to the extent that there is such repetition of experience, without its being necessarily the case that we abstract the principle from experience; for the experience may be merely the cause or necessary condition of our recognition of the principle. There are obvious difficulties about the idea that we come to recognise *all* principles in this way, since some principles may be inferred or otherwise derived from others. Aristotle saw this point when he put forward his account as one of how we come to know *first* principles. Let us accept that point for the sake of argument. There are still many difficulties that remain to be faced.

In the first place, the account is almost totally *a priori*. We can know little or nothing empirically about the frequency with which individuals have experience of given items, let alone of the relative frequency with which they have experience of them in comparison with other people. For all we know it might be predictable on this kind of basis that different people will come to quite different principles of classification from others. Yet in fact we have common principles of classification and common knowledge about what is so. Indeed knowledge *must* be public and common in this sense. On the account under consideration it is difficult, if not impossible, to allow for that fact, since it presupposes that arriving at principles is something that the individual does by himself. There is no place in the account for other people, or at least the agreement that we can have with others when we have knowledge remains unexplained. Any such agreement could not be more than mere coincidence, and it might even be said that it remains obscure what it is that agreement with others could really amount to. If agreement over what is so is to be set down as more than coincidence, the only place in which a proponent of this account can look for explanation is in the similarity between men and the similarity in which they live. That a sufficient similarity exists for these purposes is doubtful. Hence while I do not think that this would be a sufficient explanation it broaches issues that would entail the desertion of a strict empiricism. For the development of experience would then turn not simply on how it happens to fall but also on what we are born with. Even so the community of experience and knowledge would still not be a community of a genuine kind, one which rests on genuine inter-subjective agreement.

Noam Chomsky has raised a difficulty of a somewhat different kind in the course of his criticism of B. F. Skinner's account of language learning, and it is a point to which he has attached considerable importance in his other writings on these matters. It would be as well to consider it at this stage. The point rests in one way on empirical issues, but it also has certain conceptual implications. Skinner, as a behaviourist, believes that language learning can be construed solely in terms of the building up of linkages between items in experience. The linkages in question are constituted by Skinner's own brand of conditioning: operant conditioning. In this, repetition plays a large part, as it does in conditioning in general, but it is not the only factor since motivational considerations also come into the picture. In operant conditioning so-called,[7] an operant is a form of behaviour 'emitted' by an animal rather than called out from it by a stimulus. It can be perpetuated in a given situation (e.g., lever-pressing by a laboratory rat in a 'Skinner box' so as to produce pellets of food) by suitably rewarding the performance, so that the behaviour is linked thereby to the situation. Skinner thinks that all behaviour, including verbal behaviour, is learnt in this way and is thus capable of being explained by reference to this. Chomsky's reply in effect involves two connected points. First, he lays emphasis on the creativity of language, the possibility, as Von Humboldt put it, of putting finite means to infinite ends, or as we might say, of continually saying new things by old means, so that it seems highly unlikely, to say the least, that verbal behaviour could be broken down into a series of atomic items linked together in the way that Skinner supposes. Second (and this is really a connected point), the individual child does not on learning to speak have sufficient experience of language-use in what it hears from others to enable it to get from this all the rules of language (grammatical rules) that it has to come to employ. This is a connected point because it is related to the point that the verbal behaviour that it learns to perform cannot be analysed into a set of discrete but linked items which could be built up by means of any process akin to conditioning.

I shall return to this point and to its consequences in the next chapter, when considering Chomsky's own views. It is relevant in the present context because it seems that it can be generalised. When so generalised it is akin to the criticisms that Piaget has in mind with reference to empiricism when he describes it as genesis without structure. Chomsky believes that there must be something that is capable of structuring the 'information' that the child receives, a set of 'hypotheses' which the child can apply to the data so as to construct for himself the rules that he must follow in language-use. I do not wish at the moment to make any comment on this way of putting the issue, though I think it very misleading, to say the least. The real point at issue can nevertheless be put by saying that the child must, so to speak, contribute something of his own to the learning process; he cannot be viewed merely as the passive recipient of influences from the environment. I do not mean by this to suggest that the child must necessarily be active in the sense of actively engaging in a process of discovery, though this may be to some extent and at certain times true, and the activity of the child has been much emphasised by, for example, Piaget. All that need be implied in the point at stake is that the child's eventual competence is not a simple product of environmental influences; the child may, perhaps must, be determined in the way that he learns at least in part by what he is in himself, even if this is construed in such a way as to be limited to his physiological make-up. Chomsky sometimes refers in the context of the acquisition of linguistic competence to a 'language acquisition device', a device, no doubt part of our physiology, which is capable of utilising, by a process of structuring, the 'information' received, in the way that a programmed computer can utilise information fed into it. Our brains are no doubt language acquisition devices in this sense, although they are also much else, and Chomsky believes that language competence is specific and requires a specific acquisition device.

The reference to a computer is in many ways apposite in this context. Programming is in effect a form of structuring, and the way in which a computer is programmed structures the way in which any subsequent information received can be utilised. I do not mean to suggest by this that one can necessarily gain an understanding of learning by considering computing. Computers can produce new information from whatever has been received by them according to the way in which they have been programmed. Whether or not it would be right to call this 'learning' depends in part on whether it is right to attribute learning to non-conscious entities. But if objections on that score were waived it would be no less right (and no more right either) to speak of a computer as having learnt something than it was to speak of Meno's boy in the geometrical example of that dialogue as having learnt what is the length of side of a square twice the area of a given square. As I said in the first chapter, not all learning is like that, but it is a form of learning all the same. To the extent that the issues of the *Meno* can be generalised they underwrite the point that learning in general and cognitive development in particular presuppose and depend upon a pre-existent structure. The question that remains is whether that is all that there is to it. When Piaget claims that in the context of cognitive development genesis involves structure he means more than that, and he would repudiate the suggestion that it is enough to rely on the idea of a *pre-existent* structure. I shall return to this point in a later chapter. At present it is enough to note that what is common to the criticisms of empiricism brought forward by both Chomsky and Piaget is that it is implausible to suppose that learned behaviour is built up from a series of discrete items linked together through experience in just the way that experience takes us. It is implausible because when one reflects upon the concepts in terms of which the business is properly to be understood it becomes apparent that it *could not* happen like that.

The last point is in effect made by Chomsky when he says that for the study of language learning what is important is not the performance of speakers but their competence. The point could be made in other ways by saying that what Skinner presents is a theory of animal behaviour in which what an animal does when it has learnt to behave in a certain way is construed as, at best, the product of a series of habits or dispositions, and, at worst, if the theory is taken seriously, the product of a series of causally connected reactions. It is this last idea which underlies the suggestion that learning is explicable in terms of conditioning, even if the conditioning in question is of the kind that Skinner calls 'operant conditioning' and is not based simply on the substitution of one stimulus for another, as is supposed to be the case in so-called classical conditioning. (I have indicated in the paper 'Conditioning and Behaviour' (see note 7, ch. 2)—and this has been suggested by other writers also, including Skinner himself—that the *theory* of classical Pavlovian conditioning, which depends essentially on the idea of stimulus substitution, does not actually get an application to the Pavlovian experimental situation, and that it is doubtful whether classical conditioning ever really occurs. Operant conditioning so-called is not really similar enough to classical conditioning to deserve the title 'conditioning'.)

But when an animal learns to do something it really comes to *know how* to do that thing; not, be it noted, that it simply comes to be able to do that thing, since coming to be able to do something may not be the result of learning, and many animals can do things, even things that they could not do when born, as the result of maturation without learning coming into it in any way. The point is that there is an intimate connection between the concepts of knowledge and learning, which it is part of my aim to bring out. Chomsky's point about linguistic competence could be made in other ways by saying that what the child has to do, and normally does, is to acquire in some way the knowledge how to speak the language which those in his environment use. He has, of course, to do more than that: he has to come to know how to understand what those people say and to know how to respond to them in a variety of ways. But knowing how is crucial. (I shall in chapter 9 indicate how this is to be reconciled with the fact that we do sometimes speak of learning where the relevance of knowing how is not immediately obvious, e.g., learning to see things in certain ways, or even learning bad habits.)

Ryle, who in modern times has been chiefly responsible for the distinction between knowing how and knowing that,[8] has emphasised the points that knowing how cannot be reduced to knowing that and that the latter may presuppose the former. Whatever may be said about the latter point, what I have said about the difference between knowing how to do something and merely being able to do it suggests the importance of making clear the way in which knowing how constitutes knowledge. I think that an ability to do something is a case of knowing how to the extent that the person or animal has knowledge of the principle involved. If I know the principle involved in a certain performance I shall be able to repeat or carry out that performance in a variety of circumstances, even perhaps despite obstacles, by modifying my behaviour accordingly. It is this, indeed, which marks off a skill. Knowledge of the principles involved in a particular skill does not entail being able to state or formulate those principles. Indeed, in some cases the only grounds for the conclusion that someone does know certain principles may be the behaviour that he manifests in the exercise of the skill. Many people know how to do things which they have learnt to do without being able to say what is involved; indeed, in some cases making explicit to oneself the principles involved may inhibit the skill in question. I am told that if one made explicit to oneself the principles involved in turning a corner on a bicycle one would fall off, and I suspect that analogous things are true of the principles involved in knowing how to use language. What all this implies is that if learning to do something involves coming to know how to do it, and if this in turn involves in some way knowledge of the principles involved, a necessary part of any theory of learning to do things will involve a story about the acquisition of knowledge of principles. This is foreign to any theory of the kind that Skinner presents. It is for this reason that Skinner's theory is not merely false to the facts; it could not do what is required of it if it is to be a theory of *learning*.

This reference to knowledge of principles brings us back in effect to the kind of issues involved in my discussion of Aristotle. It is possible to sum up the situation by saying that even if *some* knowledge of principles comes about because our attention is drawn to them through repetition of cases in which they are applied in our experience, this cannot be the way in which all such knowledge comes about, nor the way in which such knowledge comes about at all in the first instance. Next, what is in fact repeated within our experience seems entirely contingent, so that this kind of account could not provide a sure and adequate explanation of any regular way in which knowledge develops. Last, it does not explain how it is possible to speak of the development of *our* knowledge, how, that is, inter-personal or inter-subjective agreement arises, nor how objectivity comes about. I shall return to some of these issues later.

3   Structure without genesis

When Piaget speaks of theories which involve the idea of structure without genesis he probably has in mind Gestalt Theory in particular; for the Gestaltists have laid great weight on nativism as opposed to empiricism (to use the terms employed by Wolfgang Köhler, one of the leading proponents of that theory). I have discussed that movement and its origins elsewhere,[1] and I shall not repeat that discussion here, as it is not strictly relevant to my present concerns. In the context of learning the Gestaltists have emphasised such notions as that of 'insight', a notion which has some similarity to Aristotle's notion of 'intuition'. In employing that idea they have sought to oppose the empiricist view that I discussed in the last chapter: that learning is simply a matter of the building up of linkages or connections between atomic items. They have also laid great weight upon the role played by principles of structure in the genesis of insight. That is to say that they have emphasised the tendency of the mind, whether human or animal, to see things in terms of whole structures or *gestalten*, rather than in terms of individual items which can be additive only. Such tendencies are due, in their view to the innate structuring of the mind, due in turn to innately determined brain structures. The Gestaltists have always played down the part or role performed by the contingencies of experience in human and animal development, and their view is thus rightly set against the view discussed in the last chapter. It would, of course, be impossible to discount the role of experience altogether in any such theory, but this does not rule out the possibility of viewing experience merely as providing the occasion for the application of principles of structure, rather than as the source or cause of such principles. On this view experience would function merely as a catalyst, so to speak. In so far as they accept such a view, it is thus not unfair to say that the Gestaltists embrace the idea of structure without genesis; for according to that view there is in experience no true development or progression, merely the working out of what is already implicit in the innate structures.

In effect this would be to construe learning as in all cases of the pattern represented by the *Meno*'s geometrical example. In that, as we have already seen, the boy learns the solution of the problem by making explicit to himself what is implied by and was implicit in the things that he already knew. I described Plato's theory of this as a variation on rationalism, but the pattern of knowledge acquisition presupposed is in fact typical of rationalist thinking in general. It assimilates all knowledge to *a priori* knowledge, knowledge that can be acquired without being derived from experience. To the extent that such knowledge could be thought of as new, it would typically involve, as I have already said, the working out of the consequences of what is already known, in the way in which one may come to a new piece of mathematical knowledge from what one already knows of mathematical principles. It should be noted, however, that this account of the way in which new mathematical knowledge may come about does not imply that the knowledge of the mathematical principles themselves need be in any sense innate, any more than the fact that a piece of knowledge is *a priori* implies in general that it is innate. To say that certain knowledge is not derived from experience does not imply that one must be born with it, for, as Kant pointed out, while all knowledge may come *with* experience it may not all come *from* experience. Experience may be the occasion for our coming to know something without its being the case that we get the knowledge from experience. There has nevertheless been a tendency within rationalist thinking to suppose that there must be innate knowledge, and innate ideas also, if it is possible to distinguish the one from the other. (Leibniz, who is thought of as the rationalist who espoused the cause of innate ideas *par excellence*, explained what it is to have an idea in terms of knowledge.)

Suppose, however, that we do have innate knowledge, what role does subsequent experience play in relation to this? Plato's answer, it will be remembered, was that experience reminds us of the knowledge that we already have but do not remember. When this is stripped of the mythology it amounts to the thesis that experience makes explicit what is until that moment only implicit. It must surely be along these lines that the answer to my question must be sought; for what one experiences must be at least an exemplification of what one knows in other ways. Indeed with certain kinds of knowledge it may seem at least doubtful whether one should use the term 'knowledge' until the exemplification in experience is attained. I have in mind here knowledge of such things as the colour of objects and what it is for things to be of that colour. In the last chapter I referred to the difficulties involved in the idea that one obtains the knowledge of what it is for something to be red from sense-experience; the main point is that much else would have to be known already for this to be possible in any sense. In the present context, however, the additional knowledge is not the problem. One might be able to presume an innate knowledge of the structural relationships between colours (the sort of knowledge that even a blind man might have); one might even presume *some* knowledge of what a colour is, e.g., that colours extend over the surfaces of objects, that they are perceptible by means of the eyes, and that they possess or may possess properties such as saturation, analogous to the saturation of a solution. There is a sense, however, in which one might say that a blind man (or at any rate one born blind) has no *real* knowledge of what it is for things to be coloured; the crucial factor of having had experience of colours is missing from the sort of account of knowledge of colour that I have given so far. The same would apply to the innate knowledge that I was considering; until this is exemplified in experience it is feasible to say that it could not be *real* knowledge. Such difficulties do not, of course, apply to all knowledge, only to that which involves perception in an intimate way; or at any rate it is only in such cases that the difficulties arise in a crucial form. The point does suggest, however, that not all knowledge as we understand it could possibly be innate, or even be a candidate for being innate. Experience is required for knowledge to have one or other kind of particularity; not just the kind of particularity involved in knowing what it is for something to be of a particular colour, but also, for example, that involved in knowing something to be at a particular place at a particular time. Experience enters in various ways into our identification of particulars, but in ways which it need not enter while our concern is with general truths, even if in the end experience is involved there too. There is this much truth at least in Aristotle's claim that experience is concerned with particulars.

One might put the point by saying that we need experience to give us knowledge of the ways in which abstract knowledge otherwise obtained is to be exemplified and made concrete. It is not just that abstract knowledge needs application to concrete particulars; one must get to know through experience *how* that abstract knowledge gets application. Thus it is not enough for Plato to say that experience reminds us of what we already know, even if we are content with the attempt to solve his problem within his own terms. We need to know also *how* it so reminds us. It is perhaps of interest that when Plato reinvokes his doctrine of recollection in the *Phaedo* (72e ff.), to explain how we can have knowledge of abstract and ideal notions like that of equality (i.e. the Forms) when we have never met with perfect or ideal equality in experience, he does suppose that there are ways in which the reminder functions. For he leads up to the doctrine by spelling out some of the principles which have become part of the doctrine of the association of ideas; that we may pass from one idea to another if there is an association between the two because of their similarity or if there is a contrast between them or contiguity in experience. We need not accept the view than when, to use Plato's example, we see equal sticks and stones, which are in one way or another imperfectly equal, we are reminded of perfect equality, knowledge of which we were born with even if we have forgotten it, in order to see that it is necessary for us to understand something of the ways in which the mathematical idea of equality can get application in experience, where it does not apply unequivocally.

What is in effect the same issue was raised by Kant in that part of the *Critique of Pure Reason* concerned with what he called the doctrine of the schematism. There he speaks of a certain power hidden in the depths of the human soul, a power which is in some way a function of the imagination and is the power of giving exemplification in experience to abstract principles or concepts. For this purpose, Kant thinks, we need what he calls a schema, something that gives us a rule for applying formal or abstract principles and concepts to cases, a role which in the case of empirical principles and concepts can be performed by something like an image and is for this reason a function of the imagination. The power or rule is hidden in the depths of the human soul since the ability to apply a principle or concept to cases is not something that takes the form of explicitly formulated knowledge of a principle of application. If I know in a formal way what a dog is (if, that is, I could in principle provide a formal definition of the term 'dog'), I do not necessarily thereby know how to identify dogs in practice, although presumably I shall not really know what a dog is until I can do something in that direction. To do that, however, I do not have to have explicit knowledge of a set of formal rules of the kind 'A dog is an animal which looks ... '. It is just that in learning through experience what a dog is and is like I shall learn to identify dogs. If anyone wishes to say that one thereby learns implicitly the rules for identifying dogs, there is no great harm in this as long as one does not think of this on the analogy of explicit and formulated knowledge. In the case of some concepts (e.g., once again that of 'red') it is to say the least unclear how such rules could be formulated; but one normally has no difficulty in

31

identifying red things, provided that one has learnt to do so via the appropriate form of sense-perception and provided that conditions are not abnormal.

A similar point to this one is in effect made by Chomsky, although it is not clear that he himself recognises it as such. As I indicated in the last chapter, Chomsky suggests that the data available to the child in his experience are insufficient for him to be able to abstract linguistic or grammatical rules from them. The data are in that sense corrupt. He thinks that since for that reason empiricism will not work the only course is to posit innate knowledge of the basic principles of language, what he calls the deep structure of language. Without going into the details of what the deep structure is supposed to be, it can be said that knowledge of it must include all that is basic to the ability to use language, a knowledge of what basically it is to talk, a basic linguistic competence. It will thus include the knowledge of what it is for something to be a subject, or what things are said about, and also what it is for things to be said about this—in other words, the ideas of subject and predicate. (I leave aside for the moment the terms of reference under which the problem is set up: the idea of the child's having to make something of data with which it is confronted. There is something very wrong with this idea, but I shall return to it later at another point.)

If we accept for the sake of argument, although only for this, the fundamental position that there is innate knowledge of the deep structure of language, it should be clear that this knowledge can be formal only; it cannot bring with it any knowledge of its application to cases. The child does after all have to *learn* to talk in the way that others in its environment do. Chomsky does not in the least suppose that the child is born with a complete knowledge of all languages; nor does he suppose with Plato that the child simply has to be reminded of what he in effect already knows. He does, however, have to explain how the child learns to apply the formal knowledge of language to cases, in that the child has to learn how the basic linguistic ideas are expressed and given flesh in the particular language that he is learning. Hence, Chomsky supposes that what the child learns in experience is a set of transformational rules by means of which the basic knowledge of deep structure is mapped on to the surface structure of the actual language which he is learning. The task of linguistics is to make those rules explicit. The rules in question (and there will be others dealing with the semantic or phonetic aspects of language) are in effect rules for identifying the surface structures of language as instances of underlying deep structures.

Is it, however, the case that the child has to learn such rules any more than he has to learn rules for identifying dogs or red things? To ask that question is not to ask whether he has to learn to identify forms of language in the sense that he has to know what they are in use. It is to ask whether *that* is suitably expressed in terms of the learning of rules. As I said earlier, there may be no harm in putting things in that way as long as it is not taken as implying anything analogous to explicit and formulated knowledge. The linguist may be able, and indeed should seek to be able, to formulate such rules in his theory of the language, but that does not imply that the speaker need know the rules in the same way. Indeed, as is pointed out by Theodore Mischel,[2] the speaker does not need to know the linguist's rules any more than the bicycle-rider needs to know the physical principles which govern his performance; as I suggested at the end of the last chapter conscious reliance upon such rules may inhibit performance to the extent of making it impossible. It has indeed been suggested that the answer to the question 'What does the speaker know?' is 'Nothing'.[3] The answer may not be quite right or may at least be an exaggeration, but it is certainly true that the speaker does not need to know the grammatical rules that govern the language in an explicit way, and it might well hamper him if he were too conscious of them—a point which may have some implications for the teaching of grammar.

Let us be content, therefore, with the conclusion that learning to apply abstract knowledge to cases through experience is not happily expressed in terms of learning further rules. That does not exclude the possibility that experience may *sometimes* prompt us to make more explicit what we know implicitly in a way that makes reference to rules plausible; similar considerations apply to connecting something that one knows with other things that one knows. In so far, however, as experience gives rise to new knowledge which is not simply implicit in what one already knows it is not plausible to put this in terms of the learning of rules. On the other hand, the scope for new knowledge, on the theory that we are considering, is very limited; it is restricted to the particularisation and concretisation of abstract knowledge that one already has, through application to cases. This fact is not affected by the point that in some cases one cannot really be said to know X unless one knows it in its concrete application. It is in this sense that the theory remains one that embraces the idea of structure without genesis; no really new structures come into being, only modifications of what already exists. The situation is thus parallel, as Piaget has suggested, to the theory of preformation in biology, according to which the structure of organisation in the germ-plasm dictates the subsequent development of the organism, to which the course of experience can contribute only marginal influences other than providing the occasion for the development. In that case experience merely promotes the development of what is already there and on lines determined by what is already there. Piaget wants to put in place of that conception of the matter the idea of 'epigenesis', a notion taken from C. H. Waddington; according to this conception development arises out of a strictly conceived interaction between organism and environment, without the assumption made by empiricism that the organism is entirely plastic. (Piaget sometimes assimilates empiricism to Lamarckianism, innatism to orthodox neo-Darwinianism.)

It might be objected, however, that a theory such as Chomsky's does more than this, in that it does more than present a view of experience which makes it simply promote the development of what is already there and determined. That account of the matter might apply to Plato, even when his initial view is supplemented by a story about the ways in which we are reminded of what we already know. It does not, however, apply to any view that maintains that through experience we learn the rules which connect what we already know with the particulars with which we are confronted in experience. I think that such an objection would be fair. It *is* important to distinguish a Chomsky-type view, according to which experience does play a role in the growth of new knowledge, even if that new knowledge is restricted in scope, from a view which gives experience the role of a catalyst or releaser of knowledge only. It nevertheless seems clear that unless a rationalist in his approach to the development of knowledge is prepared to embrace the view that all knowledge and all ideas are really innate he must allow some role to be performed by experience and must to that extent be an incomplete rationalist. Equally he must in that case be prepared to give some account of how this element of learning by experience comes into the picture and takes place. I have noted and rejected the suggestion that the learning in question can be construed as akin to the learning of rules or indeed actually as the learning of rules. On that view it would be as if, having already the formal knowledge of what an X is, one has to learn the rules that govern the exemplification of X. That would in effect be learning the criteria for something's being an X. But while it may be true, and no doubt is true, that there are always criteria of that kind, it does not follow that one has to be able to formulate the criteria in order to be able to identify Xs. I have laboured this point already and suggested that there must come a stage in the learning at which any question of formulating criteria must be excluded. If that is so we cannot construe the learning by saying that it is of the form: knowing in a formal and abstract way what an X is and then learning what makes an X an X.

I put the matter in this way because it seems to me that there are grounds for thinking that this is how Chomsky is inclined to take it. I have already referred to the idea that the language-learner has to acquire knowledge of the rules that connect deep structure with surface structure. On pp. 76ff of *Language and Mind* (first edition) Chomsky speaks of the child arriving at hypotheses about the language which he is learning, and he goes on to discuss as relevant to what the child has to do Peirce's idea of abduction; the process of selecting the best hypothesis to explain the facts in the context of theory-construction. The business is complicated, he says, because the child not only has to learn correct ways of speaking but also to learn which sentences are 'ill-formed, deviant, fragmentary and so on'. Thus 'formally speaking, the learner must select a hypothesis regarding the language to which he is exposed that rejects a good part of the data on which this hypothesis must rest' (p. 77). Hence, learning the rules is to be construed, on this view, in terms of putting forward hypotheses in a complicated situation and subjecting them to the process of testing, in order to see whether they provide the best account of the data. It is surely very strange to suppose that the child has to engage in this sort of activity, even formally speaking. Behind this supposition lie, I think, two ideas, the first of which at least Chomsky acknowledges and indeed emphasises: (a) that if data are to be intelligible as such, and therefore worth calling data, they must be approached with a prior and limited set of hypotheses; and (b) that learning from experience is a matter of making sense of the data provided by experience in terms of hypotheses dictated by what one already knows. Chomsky further construes the latter as a matter of coming to know what are the rules that connect what one already knows with what one comes to know if the data are interpreted in terms of the hypotheses. That is to say that making sense of the data in terms of prior hypotheses is interpreted as a matter of understanding the rules connecting what is known before the business gets going (the deep structure) with what is known as a result of it (the surface structure). I have already criticised that idea. I wish now to attend to the first point and some of its consequences.

That data must be approached with a prior set of hypotheses if they are to be intelligible as such has been suggested often enough by philosophers, particularly those who wish to oppose the idea that data can be absolute so that we can be given information in experience in an absolute and unconditioned way, without reference to anything else (an idea, of course, that goes with the suggestion that there are sense-data which provide the foundations of knowledge). If experience in general is to be construed in this way—in terms of the setting up and testing of hypotheses—it is evident that the hypotheses would have to exist for the learner prior to any experience. Hence this conception must take one on the royal road to innate ideas and innate knowledge, and this must apply to all forms of knowledge to which experience is relevant, not merely some of them. Those who take this view of experience have generally been influenced by writers on the philosophy of science, where the suggestion that knowledge grows and comes about through the putting of questions (hypotheses) to nature has a certain plausibility. As applied to the growth of knowledge in the individual, however, the idea has the consequence of making the child into something like a little scientist. This is evident in Chomsky's way of setting out the issue, when he speaks of the child having to discover the grammar of the language and of his putting forward hypotheses about the rules that have to be followed. Even if this were plausible, however, it would have the further consequence that the child would in that case be a solitary investigator of his environment. The view that this is how it is falls in with a considerable tradition in western epistemology, according to which the problems of knowledge are essentially problems for an individual consciousness which is faced with the task of constructing its world by deciding which of its experiences, if any, are in any sense objective. There are reasons why the problems of epistemology have often been formulated in this fashion, stemming from Descartes's method of doubt and his concentration on what are for the conscious thinking self clear and distinct ideas. The problems as so formulated are thus intimately connected with the issues inherent in Cartesian dualism and its suggestion that one should start epistemology with the 'I think'. Chomsky's espousal of rationalism is a reinforcement of that tradition.

It is clear from certain remarks in *Language and Mind* that Chomsky's espousal of innate knowledge is not restricted to the field of language. He suggests there (p. 68) that the task of accounting for human knowledge is the classical problem of psychology, and he stresses what he calls the enormous disparity between knowledge and experience. Earlier (p. 64) he asks in what areas of human competence one might hope to see developed a theory analogous to that of generative grammar. He suggests as two speculative possibilities 'the problem of how a person comes to acquire a certain concept of three-dimensional space or an implicit "theory of human action" '. It is of some interest that the concept of space is one of those concepts that have often been taken to be *a priori*, while the concept of human action is certainly often taken to be a concept that cannot be reduced to anything like the concept of observable bodily movement. In fact, if one were to ask how the child acquires the idea of action from what it observes of its environment, one would indeed be confronted with a problem that looks insuperable. If it is supposed that the child asks himself what determines whether something in his environment is performing an action, we are not only confronted with the problem of how he gets the idea of action in the first place, but we are also faced with something like the classical other-minds problem. As is well known to philosophers who have concerned themselves with that problem, there is nothing in what happens that will tell one that it is an action, since action implies also intention of some kind on the part of the actor, and this presupposes also mentality on his part. Thus, if action implied mentality, the question 'Is that an action?' is of a part with the question 'Is that something that has a mind?'. There seems no hope of getting the idea of action or the knowledge of the conditions under which it is properly to be applied simply from what one observes. It might well seem, therefore, that if the problem is approached from this starting-point an *a priori* idea of action is inescapable, so that the concept of action falls into line in this respect with that of space. Even so, if the task of experience is to bring about the knowledge of what counts as action, there remain great difficulties as to how it is possible, as my reference to the other-minds problem indicates.

All three problems—those of the knowledge of language, knowledge of space, knowledge of action—seem capable of being structured similarly. As Chomsky sees them, the problems start from the idea that knowledge of what the thing in question is (language, space, action) could not be derived directly from experience; the role of experience is simply to give application to the ideas, which we have independently. Construed in this way each theory seems to imply that there exists innate knowledge. I say 'construed in this way' because it is at this point that the Kantian thesis that while all knowledge may come through experience it does not necessarily come from experience becomes

37

pertinent. The fact, if it is one, that a certain item of knowledge is *a priori* does not entail that it must be innate. To escape the conclusion that it must be innate we should, of course, have to construe the role that these ideas have in the growth of knowledge rather differently from that which Chomsky gives to them. We should not be able to say in each case that we gain from experience knowledge of what makes an X an X, given already, and prior to all experience, some kind of knowledge of what an X is. At the least we should have to think of both forms of knowledge coming together in some way. There is no need, therefore, to posit innate knowledge to deal with the problem how knowledge connected with so-called *a priori* ideas is to be thought of as coming about.[4]

On the other hand, the adoption of the view that empirical knowledge is *always* the result of putting up hypotheses and deciding which of them best explains the data makes any reliance upon a distinction between *a priori* and other ideas (so-called *a posteriori* ideas) beside the point. In *every* case if the hypotheses are to be intelligible to us they must presuppose knowledge and understanding on our part, prior to experience. This would have the effect, as we have already seen, of enforcing adoption of the view that there is innate knowledge corresponding to *every* item of empirical knowledge acquired. The role of innate knowledge could not be restricted to cases where the ideas involved are *a priori*. *Every* case of the acquisition of knowledge of what makes an X an X or of what constitutes being an X will presuppose, on this view, prior and therefore, ultimately, innate knowledge of a formal and abstract kind of what an X is. Hence the solution that Chomsky adopts to what he has called 'the classical problem of psychology' must be seen as quite general; and that fact may rob it of any attractiveness it may have in areas where the nature of the ideas involved may seem to make an empiricist view of the situation particularly implausible. The complete generality of a theory of innate ideas, the fact that it would have to postulate innate knowledge of everything, the idea of which is subsequently cashed in experience, would inevitably undermine the case for its acceptability, even if it were acceptable on other grounds. I shall return to the issue and a different kind of objection to a theory of innate knowledge in a later chapter.

In addition there are the difficulties that we have already noted as inherent in the second of the two main ideas that I attributed to Chomsky: that the acquisition of new knowledge is a matter of making sense of the particular data provided by experience in terms of hypotheses dictated by what one previously knows. I have noted the temptation to think that this can be construed as the learning of rules. Even when the objection is waived that not all learning is a matter of coming to be able to identify particular items in terms of previously known universals or general truths, it remains the case that the identification of particulars in this way cannot be construed in terms of, or at least not simply in terms of, the learning of rules. For rules are inevitably general in form; they connect things construed as such and suches, and they cannot justify or explain their application to the particulars which are by that application so construed. Experience must somehow provide the basis for application to particulars of knowledge which is otherwise general in form. To put the matter in other words, even if it is true that the ultimate intelligibility of data depends upon their being approached with a prior hypothesis, there must be some access to the data which is independent of that hypothesis. Unless, that is, we presuppose that there is some form of knowledge of particulars which is independent of the abstract and general hypotheses, and which can be used to test or assess the applicability of the hypotheses to the particulars, the method so conceived cannot get off the ground. This is quite apart from the question whether all learning can be construed in these terms in any case.

Thus anyone who accepts that experience must have some epistemological role must be an imperfect rationalist and an incomplete believer in innatism, to say the least. The only other course that is possible is to construe experience in such a way that it is not given an epistemological role, so that it is not an independent source of knowledge. This might be done, for example, by construing experience as in some way merely the *cause* through which implicit knowledge is made explicit. We saw that in Plato's doctrine of recollection it has this role, at any rate in the *Meno*, where the doctrine is not linked with the question of how ideal knowledge of such things as equality can be given application to an imperfect experience. In the *Meno* experience is given the role merely of reminding us of what we once knew; experience merely triggers off the resuscitation of that knowledge. It is of interest too that in order to make this the sole account of how learning is possible, Plato has to preface it with the suggestion that the soul has long ago seen everything. Thus every item of knowledge that we now have, of whatever form, is simply a resuscitation of that same knowledge that we have had before. If that same knowledge was similarly acquired an infinite regress must result. This would be fatal to the theory, even if it were not implausible in other ways.

For rationalism, therefore, there is something of a dilemma. Either some knowledge is after all derived from experience and we are then faced with the problem of how it fits in with that knowledge which is supposedly innate; or all knowledge is innate, and we are then faced with the problem of how experience functions in some purely causal way so as to resuscitate the knowledge which is innate but can scarcely be supposed to be explicit. It is clear that Plato's suggestion that 'reminding' could be thought of as playing what is in effect a causal role will not in the end do. He himself admits in the *Phaedo* that when X reminds us of Y it is either because of a similarity of dissimilarity that we know to exist between X and Y, or because what we know of X is connected in some other way with what we know of Y. Thus the notion of being reminded of something cannot be understood without reference to knowledge in some way; it is not a purely causal notion. That is not to say that the idea of our being caused to have knowledge of something lacks intelligibility altogether (although this has often been supposed to be the case by recent philosophers); rather it is to say that in the present case it is unintelligible how experience could be supposed to cause us to have knowledge, unless the whole thing could be seen against a further epistemological background. In fact most rationalists have been incomplete rationalists and have indeed supposed that some knowledge is derived from experience.

It would seem to follow from all this that if the idea of structure without genesis is taken literally it can constitute an extreme or ideal case only. In this it may seem to compare unfavourably with genesis without structure, which has seemed to many much more plausible and probably true. Most of us are impressed by the place that experience has in our lives and we may well be tempted to suppose that it is all-pervasive. Environment is all, or so it may seem. Further reflection, however, may well suggest that this cannot literally be true. The human and animal nervous system, and physiological system generally, is a complex system; it would be very surprising if it were completely plastic and did not of itself determine to some extent or other the ways in which environmental influences affect us. It would be surprising if much about ourselves were not innately determined. That, however, does not necessarily imply the existence of innate *knowledge*. That notion arises only if the growth of understanding in relation to experience is construed in a certain way, roughly, as we have seen, in terms of the individual putting questions to his environment, something that presupposes prior knowledge and understanding if the idea is to be intelligible. There is no need to construe the situation in that way, but, if one does not, an alternative account of the growth of experiential knowledge seems to be demanded. I shall return to that question later (see especially chapter 7), and at the same time I shall adduce a consideration that suggests that the notion of innate knowledge, so far from being plausible, is not even really intelligible. The consideration is based on the idea that having knowledge implies having a concept of truth; this in turn implies as its criterion agreement with others in some way, so that it gets no purchase in a context where such agreement is ruled out. Moreover, that agreement must be a real agreement and not just a matter of coincidence, as it would be if it were simply the case that one was born with beliefs that happened to agree with those of others. None of these conditions seems to be satisfied or to be satisfiable in the case of the putative innate knowledge. What I have now said, however, is merely the skeleton of an argument and not the argument itself. I shall return to the argument itself later.

The objections to which I shall now turn, those that flow from the theory that Piaget presents, are of a different kind and take as their point of departure the idea that genesis with structure is the correct way of depicting the facts. Here the parallel to be sought within classical epistemology is the philosophy of Kant, who similarly attempted to provide a third way between rationalism and empiricism.

4   Genesis with structure

If there has been a tendency on the part of some, as I noted in the last chapter, to view the child simply as a young adult, with more or less adult thought processes, this has never been a tendency attributable to Piaget. Quite the reverse. Piaget has always emphasised the point that we must not attempt to construe a child's mind simply in terms of what we know of adults, and that emphasis has been extremely salutary. He has in fact taken the matter even further and claimed that we cannot really understand adult thought processes unless we see how they emerge from those of the child. It is in these terms, for example, that he has criticised Russell's definition of number, as an attempt to elucidate the concept of number along logical lines. The basis of his criticism is that Russell's account of that concept does not correspond to the facts about the way in which it emerges in the development of the thought of the individual. Piaget has emphasised that kind of point repeatedly, and it is hard to see that it rests on anything else but a misconception. Whatever Russell was doing in defining the concept of number in terms of class-correspondence, he was not claiming that thinking in terms of the concept of number emerges out of thinking about classes and their correspondence. Nor, I think, is it right to suggest that a philosophical elucidation of a concept must presuppose an account of how that concept is acquired, if only for the reason that while there may be typical ways in which a form of understanding may be arrived at there need be *no one* way in which it comes about. It depends very much on the background of understanding of the individual.[1] The situation may be different in reverse: an understanding of a concept may indeed reflect upon an understanding of the possible ways in which it may be acquired.

I shall not go further into this aspect of the matter. It does not affect my present concerns, which are not with the proper conditions for a philosophical elucidation of a concept, but with the general conditions for the acquisition of concepts or the growth of understanding. Piaget offers a comprehensive theory of this, based on a very considerable array of empirical investigations and findings. Initially these were for the most part case-histories and observations of his own children, but as time has gone on he and his associates have undertaken a vast number of investigations of other kinds. The complexities both of the empirical investigations and of the theorising superimposed upon them are very great, and it would be impossible to do anything like justice to them in a short space. My aim will be, not to produce a kind of potted account of Piaget, but to give some account of his general approach together with some assessment of it. It is difficult in any case to sort out the strictly empirical from the theoretical framework, let alone the philosophical presuppositions, and some might think it a mistake to try to do this, although I do not think this myself. Perhaps the most notable and best-known of Piaget's 'findings' is the sorting out of the distinct stages through which a child passes (and according to the theory *must* pass) in the course of cognitive development. There are three main stages, although these, especially the second, may be subdivided. They are the sensori-motor stage, which lasts until about the age of two years; the pre-operational sub-stage followed by that of concrete operations, which last until about seven years and eleven or twelve years respectively; and finally the stage of formal or abstract operations, which reaches full development by about fifteen years. The age norms may be, and have been, disputed; that does not matter for our purposes. It has often been said with some justice that there is a serious under-estimation of social and cultural influences upon the child in Piaget's thought; it is not that he ignored them altogether, it is that his theoretical interpretation of the empirical findings does not lay great weight on such considerations, especially in connection with the stages. For practical reasons the question of the validity of the age norms and whether they can be affected by cultural factors is of considerable importance. For theoretical purposes the issue is perhaps of less importance than the question of how necessary it is that the stages should follow each other in the way indicated and why.

The stages that I have noted can be roughly characterised as follows. Piaget thinks of the child as fundamentally active, rather than as functioning in a way that is the result of stimulus-response connections. The first, sensori-motor stage, which lasts until language-use appears, when there begins an interiorisation of action, is concerned with the development of manipulative and other manually skilled behaviour on the part of the young child. In the first sub-stage of the second stage (and Piaget sometimes subdivides the sub-stages yet again) the child is said not to have developed any proper concepts, although he has some facility for representation of things. The lack of proper concepts is shown in particular by the absence of the idea of reversibility, a key idea in Piaget's theorising. A path, for example, which is followed from A to B is not at this stage seen as one that connects A to B in any formal way, so that it is not seen equally as one that takes one from B to A. The absence of this idea goes together with a lack of appreciation of identity; an object is an object for the child only in connection with a given activity or operation, and it is not seen as one that may provide the focus for different operations. The best-known examples of this sort of thing are to be found in the context of the so-called conservation studies. A liquid poured from a shallow, wide glass into a narrower, tall glass is seen as being of a larger quantity in the latter case than in the former; there is thus no sense of the conservation of volume or mass, and for that reason no proper sense of the identity of things.

In the sub-stage of concrete operations there begin to emerge proper concepts associated with operations that have a logic about them: classification, ordering, seriation, and so on. But although thinking may be logical in this sense it is still concerned with concrete objects and is not divorced from them. In the final stage of formal operations thinking may become abstract, divorced from concrete objects, and may take a propositional form of a strictly logical kind. Piaget thinks that the possible transformations of propositions that are revealed in this form a 'quaternary group', the so-called INRC grouping, in which every operation implies an inverse or negation N, a reciprocal R, and a correlative which is the inverse of the reciprocal C. The relations between these are $NR = C$, $CR = N$, $CN = R$, and $NRC = I$, where I stands for identity, so that we have a kind of logic of operations based on the two fundamental ideas of inversion and reciprocity.[2] Piaget sometimes describes the whole process of development in terms of more and more complex and sophisticated structures, in the growth of which a process of decentration has taken place. By 'decentration' he means fundamentally the process of becoming less and less fixated on what is immediately before one and on what one is oneself involved in;[3] it is the inverse of the egocentricity which he sees as the main characteristic of the young child's thought. The development of intelligence through experience comes about through the building up of relations.

Piaget's thesis, therefore, is that the development of intelligence must follow a certain order, because the structures built up at a certain stage presuppose earlier structures, earlier relatings; the complex therefore presupposes the simple, the abstract the concrete. There is inevitably what Toulmin has called (see note 1, ch. 4) 'conceptual stratification', just because certain concepts logically presuppose others. If the process of growing understanding or conceptual development is thought of as a process of increasingly complex and ordered structuring of things, there should be no surprise in the suggestion that parallel or similar structures may appear either at different stages (with elements of a different order of complexity) or within a single stage (with different elements thereby systematised differently). Piaget calls these two possibilities the vertical and horizontal displacement of structures respectively. The former occurs where there are, as he puts it, filiations between structures at different ages, e.g., between the sensori-motor period and the period of concrete operations; the latter occurs when, for example, conservation of substance is assumed by the child independently of and not necessarily in connection with conservation of volume or mass. The emphasis on structure and structuring gives some kind of intelligibility to these ideas as well as to the claim that there is a natural order for the development of understanding. It thus provides one rationale for the suggestion that that order is not merely contingent.

It is clear that for Piaget it is not merely an empirical fact, discovered by him, that there are those stages in the development of understanding that he has distinguished. The theory that seeks to explain this order of development in terms of the notion of structuring brings with it the consequence that the order must be seen as in some sense necessary. Piaget admits this and welcomes the idea; indeed he criticises Freud, for example, because his view of the growth of the affective life involves the idea that it goes through stages the ordering of which is simply a matter of general fact and has no necessity about it.[4] He goes on to emphasise the point that on his view the stages of intellectual development are sequential, meaning by this (a) that the series is constant in order even if it may be speeded up or slowed down by experience or social factors, (b) that each stage is determined by a whole structure, and (c) that such a structure is 'prepared by the preceding one and integrated into the one that follows'. His thesis amounts, therefore, to the claim that in cognitive development the human mind (or, as he prefers to put it, the intelligence) relates things into more and more complex structures until it is capable of structuring those structures themselves independently of the things initially related. The question what it is that governs the structuring and determines the way in which it proceeds is something that I shall come back to, but whatever it is that does this the process is, in Piaget's eyes, a natural one.

It is not an idea that it is easy to assess, because of its great generality. If the growth of understanding can be construed in terms of structuring at all it is easy enough to accept the idea that some kinds of structure may presuppose other kinds. But is the growth of understanding to be construed in terms of structuring at all? There is also the very important point that where having one concept logically presupposes having another this has no necessary consequences for the *temporal* order of their acquisition, except that if A logically presupposes B one cannot be said to have A in the full sense *before* having B in the full sense. But it is possible for A and B to come together; alternatively, since having a concept is not an all or nothing affair, one might still have A in *some* sense or way before having B in the full sense. Thus, to use an example that I have discussed elsewhere,[5] understanding what red is (having the concept of red) logically presupposed understanding what a colour is, since being red entails being coloured. Yet could it reasonably be said that to understand what red is a person has *first* to understand all that is involved in something's being coloured? Surely understanding what it is for something to be coloured implies knowing things about how colours, including red, are related to each other and to the objects that have them. It would be impossible to teach someone what colour is and *then* teach him what red is on that basis. To suppose that one could do so is to suppose that the relations between colour concepts are all, so to speak, linear. To what extent Piaget thinks in this way is not clear. As I noted earlier, he does say that a stage is determined by a whole structure, and it might well seem that the relationship between structures at this level is in fact linear. But the situation is less clear at a less gross level.

To speak, for example, of the horizontal displacement of structures, as Piaget does in the context of the conservation studies, on the grounds that the recognition of the conservation of one feature of objects may be separated from that of the conservation of other features, makes it appear that the structures in question can be identified and compared. On that basis one could compare conservation of substance, volume, mass and so on. But features like substance, volume and mass are in fact features identified and recognised by adult (and, incidentally, educated) understanding; in coming to identify them the child is in effect acquiring an understanding of elementary physics, and in doing so he will not only identify them but also come to understand their interrelationship. Without this understanding and perhaps a good deal more besides what right has one to speak of the child's having an understanding of any one of the features?

Is it right to say of a child who, when a liquid is poured from a wide, shallow glass into a narrow, tall one, says that there is more liquid in the second, that he or she understands the principles of identity for a liquid but does not understand that a liquid retains the same volume when it is poured from one vessel into another? Does he or she really understand what volume is at all and does he or she understand what it is for a liquid to remain the same liquid? Or is the understanding of these things so partial that it is simply misleading to dignify it by speaking of it in these terms? The answers to these questions are not obvious, even when the questions are seen against the background of many other phenomena of a connected kind. Given this kind of difficulty and the vagueness that becomes apparent about how a structure is to be identified, it also becomes less than clear what kind of rationale for the theory of stages is provided in speaking of structures.

Two other kinds of rationale are apparent in what Piaget has to say, the one biological, the other philosophical. The first fits cognitive growth into a scheme of general development of a biological kind which provides a third way between the alternatives, noted in the last chapter, of preformationism and total plasticity in the face of experience. (As noted in the last chapter, Piaget sometimes discusses the matter on the level of the evolution of the species as the attempt to find a third way between Neo-Darwinianism and Lamarckianism. In both cases he appeals to C.H. Waddington as providing the third way.) The second considers the growth of knowledge as an epistemological problem, in that the task is to find a third way between empiricism and rationalism (or innatism or apriorism, as Piaget sometimes, though wrongly, calls it). Here the third way is to be found in a Kantian approach, according to which the necessity of the cognitive stages is likened to the necessity which Kant attributes to the categories in relation to human understanding. There are very evident Kantian influences at work in Piaget's thought, although Kant himself said nothing about the development or acquisition of understanding. Piaget has some tendency to identify the Kantian notion of the *a priori* with innateness, but that is quite wrong, since Kant undoubtedly thought that all knowledge arises with experience if not from experience. Another point that has to be made in this context is that Piaget also wishes to run the biological and epistemological issues together, and his book *Biology and Knowledge* is a systematic working out of that tendency. In the following I shall try to discuss the two issues separately, but I shall have from time to time to indicate the ways in which the two kinds of rationale are taken to converge.

The notions which have lived longest in Piaget's thought in connection with the biological approach are those of accommodation, assimilation and equilibration.[6] The living organism can be viewed as one which constantly interacts with its environment; it takes in and assimilates things from the environment (feeding is the most obvious example of this), and it adapts or accommodates itself to the environment. Biologically these activities have the function of producing a state of equilibrium in the organism in relation to the environment in which it finds itself, just as the functioning of bodily organs may produce a state of homeostasis in the body. Accommodation and assimilation are therefore reciprocal processes of functioning, the end-product of which should in normal circumstances be a state of equilibrium; hence their function is equilibration. Such notions, however, do not of themselves explain *development* without appeal to other features such as maturation in the organism or changes in the environment. Similar considerations apply if the same ideas are adapted to provide the biological underpinning of learning; in such a case we should have to presume that the process of equilibration brings about changes in the organism which set in motion further processes of assimilation and accommodation, or something like that. Indeed, that is how Piaget in fact views learning: as a process of equilibration in which the organism learns by actively bringing schemata to bear on the environment, with consequent feed-back and further adjustment. That way of thinking, if pursued by itself, would, however, lead one into the difficulty discussed in the last chapter, the difficulty of where the schemata come from in the first place. Moreover, while Piaget wants to leave full room for instinct, he does not want innate ideas. Thus in *The Principles of Genetic Epistemology* (p. 56) he says, 'If Chomsky is right in basing language on intelligence and not vice versa, then all we need do is to refer to sensori-motor intelligence whose structurings, prior to speech, certainly presuppose neural maturation and, even more significantly, a succession of equilibrium states proceeding by progressive coordinations and self-regulations'. So learning cannot get off the ground without maturation.

In the main, however, it is in a sense wrong to approach Piaget's theory by laying any great emphasis on the complementary ideas of maturation and learning. Piaget does invoke those ideas from time to time, but his main concern is with the general line and order of development through which the child's thought must pass. So much is this so that it has been said of him that he is a learning theorist without a learning theory.[7] If a concern with learning means a concern with how the individual benefits from experience and with the conditions that make this possible, that judgment has some truth in it. At all events, one cannot justly impose on Piaget the regress that we have seen to arise in connection with some approaches to these issues and which has its paradigm in Plato's approach in the *Meno*. The remark that I quoted above is an example of Piaget's claim that there may be filiations between earlier and later manifestations of intelligence. His criticism of Chomsky amounts to the point that it is wrong to think of the schemata which the child applies to the world in the earliest stages of its cognitive life as of the same kind as those applied later; there may be filiations or similarities of structure between them, without there being identity, and it is strict identity of structure or identity of schemata at each stage that is required if the regress is to be a real one. If for 'schema' we read 'knowledge', Piaget's point amounts to the claim that we do not need to postulate innate knowledge in Chomsky's sense, since the later knowledge emerges out of something which is in some way related to it but which is nevertheless different. This is a very important point which I shall return to and use in my own way later. As far as Piaget is concerned, and for present purposes, the important question that now arises is *how* the later states emerge out of the earlier ones with which they have filiations but not the relation of identity. What Piaget says blocks the regress in the form of it that seems blockable otherwise only by invoking innate knowledge in a full-blown sense. Nevertheless, the account seems unconscionably vague unless it is possible to explain the parts played by instinct, maturation and equilibration in the initiation of sensori-motor intelligence and how more developed intelligence arises out of this in turn.

Piaget's *Biology and Knowledge* has much to say about these issues, but the discussion is not always clear and it is in any case too complex to admit of an easy assessment. Piaget states that the two main hypotheses with which he is concerned are that 'cognitive functions are an extension of organic regulations and constitute a differentiated organ for regulating exchanges with the external world'. Hence cognitive growth is, in his opinion, based on the same principles as biological development in general. Just as Piaget thinks that cognitive development can be construed as a progressive structuring of the world, even if the structures which result may be different at different stages, so he thinks that cognitive development can be explained in terms of biological principles of a single kind, even if they work in different ways at different stages. I shall return to a consideration of this idea later;

49

at present it is necessary to note only its relevance to the problem of the regress. My present discussion stemmed from the problem of where the schemata that the organism brings to bear on the environment come from if the processes of equilibration are to get started, and how the answer to this avoids an appeal to innate knowledge. The answer has been that in effect there *is* innate knowledge but only in the sense that is involved in speaking of instinct. Hence, from the beginning there is constant interaction between the organism and the environment, involving self-regulation based on progressive equilibrium states, but this presupposes that the organism has an innate constitution which determines what is instinctual.

To account for the subsequent development (the progressive equilibrium states) Piaget invokes the idea of 'homeorhesis' which C.H. Waddington distinguishes from homeostasis. In the latter the organism reacts to any departure from a state of balance in such a way that the balance is restored. Such a notion, however, cannot in itself account for the development unless one postulates other changes in the organism or in its environment. In homeorhesis it is not a *state* of equilibrium or balance that it is the function of the system to preserve, but rather a steady course of progression, deviations from which are corrected in virtue of the self-regulating properties of the system. In the present context the system with which we are concerned is not simply the organism, but the organism in relation to the environment. The equilibrium that results from the functioning of the system is not a static one but a dynamic one, in that the functioning of the system determines a course of development governed by the progressive interaction between an organ or an organism and its environment. Waddington calls such a system an epigenetic one, and the term 'epigenesis' is one that Piaget has adopted for his own purposes. Waddington also uses the technical term 'chreod' to speak of the necessary routes that must be taken by an organ or organism in its development if the functioning of the system is to be fulfilled. Piaget sees the stages through which an individual must pass in cognitive or intellectual development as similar to these chreods. They are necessary stages in a developmental process.

Hence, to Jerome Bruner's suggestion[8] that you can teach anything to a child at any age as long as you set about it in the right way, Piaget replies that although it may be possible to speed up to some extent the passage through the stages of development, it is still necessary for the child to pass through the stages in their order. There are 'natural' ways for the mind to attain certain forms of understanding, and although it is possible to accelerate the business in local ways by special forms of teaching the overall course of development has its own necessary rhythm. For this reason Piaget thinks that there are limits to the extent to which teaching methods can accelerate the course of intellectual development, and there is an optimum length of time for this.[9] Sometimes Piaget speaks of the reference to epigenesis and chreods as the use of an analogy, but it is impossible to escape the conclusion that it is really more than this for him, and that the course of cognitive development can, in his view, really be explained throughout in terms of biological principles. If so, the influences of cultural and other social and experiential factors must indeed be local only. In sum, the individual and his environment form, in Piaget's view, an epigenetic system within which there are sequential stages the passage through which is necessary to the proper functioning of the system. Such a system can function defectively but it cannot, while it is the same system, operate so that it follows a different sequential order. It is in this spirit that we should take the words 'necessary', 'cannot', etc. that appear in claims about the stages of cognitive development.

If we turn to the epistemological strand in Piaget's thought, as distinct from the biological strand with which it is sometimes mixed, the situation may take on an appearance which is different, at any rate in some ways. As I have already noted, the two rival epistemological positions to which Piaget is opposed are empiricism and rationalism respectively, even if he does not always use those titles. The attempt to find a third way between these positions has a certain similarity to the approach of Kant to the epistemologies of the eighteenth-century empiricists and rationalists. Kant's third way or compromise between empiricism and rationalism consists in part in trying to specify certain principles of the human understanding the application of which to experience is a necessary condition if that experience is to be objective. On Kant's view this comes about because the human understanding subsumes perceptions (or intuitions, as Kant calls them) under concepts in judgment according to certain principles. Kant believes, though wrongly, that these principles can be derived from the principles of logic itself, but the important thing about them is that their application to experience in judgment is a necessary condition of the judgments in question being objective; or, as Kant sometimes puts it, of their being true for all men and not just true for me. The interaction between concepts and intuitions that lies at the basis of such objective judgments is in many ways parallel to Piaget's reciprocal processes of assimilation

51

and accommodation. The parallel might be expressed by saying that the human understanding supplies the concepts to which intuitions are assimilated, while the concepts are accommodated to the intuitions. Kant puts the matter in a famous sentence in which he says that 'thoughts without content are empty, intuitions without concepts are blind'. Hence judgment involves, on his view, a blend of intuitions and concepts, and if that judgment is to be in the running for being objective or true for all men it must conform to the *a priori* principles of which I have spoken. These principles are themselves reflections of what Kant calls 'categories', *a priori* and formal concepts under which all experience which may be called objective must fall. The necessity involved in this is a relative one in the sense that the categories and their correlative principles are necessary conditions of possible experience (where that experience is objective) and hence necessary if there is to be that experience and not otherwise.

Kant says nothing about development, since this is not his concern; he is interested, rather, in what must be the case if what we normally understand by a developed human understanding is to function as it does, in relation to experience. What Kant calls the understanding is roughly comparable to what Piaget calls the intellect, without the reference to or concern with development. It is easy to see, however, that the application of a Kantian type of thought to the developmental issue would result in a thesis properly describable as involving genesis with structure. The principles that such structuring must conform to would correspond to Kant's *a priori* principles. In his more epistemological moments Piaget sometimes speaks not of how the individual person develops cognitively but of how the *epistemic subject* develops an objective understanding of the world.[10] To put the matter in such abstract and philosophical terms suggests that he too is fundamentally concerned with the general conditions for the development of objective knowledge and understanding. To think of the matter in these terms is not to be concerned with developmental psychology as such, since the issue as so put is unrelated to what happens to any individual or set of individuals. Nor, despite some similarities, is the issue quite the same as that which was at stake when we were concerned with the biological approach; for the necessities that emerged in that context were connected with the routes that have to be followed by an item in an epigenetic system if that system is to function normally. In the present context the necessities are connected with what must happen to a knowing subject if he is to acquire, in relation to the world, knowledge and understanding that are objective.

Piaget frequently emphasises the point that in his view objectivity comes through activity,[11] by means of a progressive decentring, i.e. a progressive move away from egocentricity and thus subjectivity. Objects as they exist for the intellect are constructed by a series of approximations. Decentring of the subject and construction of reality are two sides of the same coin, subject only to the proviso that the construction of reality 'presupposes in addition a constant reference to experiences', even if the interpretation of experience itself presupposes a pre-existent schema (*Principles*, p. 82). Objectivity is thus a limit to which the epistemic subject tends, and genetic epistemology can therefore be viewed as a charting of the paths along which the subject must pass if objectivity is to be approximated to, if not attained. This thesis is Kantian to the extent that objectivity is construed as a function of the human mind and not independent of it. Perception itself is thought of in a way that is of a piece with this general point of view. Piaget does not regard it as the passive process that empiricists have generally taken it to be, and he claims (*Principles*, p. 20) that rationalists have given away too much to empiricists in this respect. 'Perception', he says (*Mechanisms*, p. 359), 'is of the *here and now* and serves the function of fitting each object or particular event into its available assimilative frameworks'. This happens, however, only to the extent that the subject is active in relation to experience. Indeed, in *The Mechanisms of Perception* he produces a theory, based on a welter of experiments on sensory illusions, which involves the claim that sensory mechanisms are naturally distorting and that it is only the processes of decentration which result from the activity (conceptual or otherwise) of the perceiver that overcome those tendencies to distortion. The evidence for this claim turns on the finding that purely sensory illusions, such as the Müller-Lyer illusion, that do not appear to be a function of any beliefs or knowledge that the perceiver has, are at their extreme in the earliest years and decrease with development. (The Müller-Lyer illusion is the one in which lines of equal length look of different length when arrow-heads facing in different directions are attached to their ends.)

Although I said earlier that 'decentration' has what is perhaps its most literal application in connection with perception, it is not at all clear that it means here quite the same as what it means in some other contexts of Piaget's thought. It involves here not so much a move away from egocentricity in the obvious sense as a ceasing to be fixated on what is immediately presented to us in perception, a ceasing to be fixated on the purely sensory, so that the intellect comes to play a larger part. The thesis that purely sensory processes are distorting seems to represent an extreme aspect of the view that objectivity is a function of activity. Kant did not say so much about intuitions, merely that without concepts they are blind. Piaget's thesis presents certain difficulties for the claim that the construction of reality presupposes a constant reference to experiences. How can this be so if the experiences, without the contribution that the epistemic subject makes, are distorting? On the other hand, without experience the structuring activity of the subject will have no basis independent of itself and in that case objectivity will, at best, amount to little more than coherence. There are strong suggestions in Piaget's thought of a point of view which amounts to just that; there are also suggestions of the idea that objectivity is commensurate with the rational or ordered. This is an implication of the connection that Piaget often makes between the notions of reversibility and objectivity; for reversibility comes very close to the idea of seeing things in all possible relations and not merely in those which initial activity on our part has determined.

These problems about objectivity give point to a general line of criticism that can be directed at Piaget. We have seen that there is a parallelism between the implications of the biological and epistemological approaches, a parallelism which makes possible the point of view on which *Biology and Knowledge* is based, that 'cognitive functions are an extension of organic regulations'; or at all events it is that parallelism which gives that point of view any plausibility that it has. One reason why the parallelism exists is that each approach treats the growth of understanding and knowledge as a function of the interaction between an individual (whether considered as organism or as epistemic subject) and his environment or world. Notions like that of objectivity have to be fitted into this framework. As far as concerns the epistemological aspects of this issue Piaget is not alone in accepting this point of view; the same could be said of the empiricist and rationalist traditions discussed earlier. Indeed all three are part of a general tradition of thought that has run through much of western philosophy, according to which epistemological problems are to be treated as a matter of whether and how the individual can construct his world. The position is perhaps most obvious in Cartesianism, which has been the source of these preconceptions in modern times. Descartes's method of doubt and the resulting 'Cogito' essentially involve the point of view that one can start from the individual's surety about his own thinking self as contrasted with his uncertainty about everything else. In that event the task of the individual is to construct his world from his own individual position. This involves a dualism in which the subject has privileged access to his own mental states, such that he can with justification be designated simply as a thinking thing, as Descartes put it. (It is perhaps worth remarking that I am not objecting to psycho-physical dualism as such, but to its epistemological version which gives priority to knowledge of one's own mental stages.) The notion of an 'external world' sums up the situation admirably in this respect; for if I am in any sense shut up in my own mental processes everything else must inevitably be external to me. By what standards can I in that case judge from my own mental processes what in that supposed external world is objective and what is not? Different philosophers have sought different answers to that question, from Descartes's clear and distinct ideas onwards.

All three theories of cognitive development that I have so far surveyed are in that tradition in one way or another. They all take the epistemological problem as one that exists for the individual in relation to his world; it is not thought of as a problem which he must of necessity share with others if only for the reason that the terms in which the problem has to be expressed have a public and therefore inter-subjective meaning. Thus the individual is not thought of as one who shares a life, both cognitive and otherwise, with others, a fact which must inevitably colour the way in which the problem of cognitive development is construed. Objects are thought of either as just there as a matter of fact, and so to be discovered (but how?), or as constructs developed by the individual (but on what principles and with what criteria of success?). The advantages of the thesis of genesis with structure over its two rivals so far considered is that it attempts to answer the questions that I have just mentioned within the terms of reference specified. It attempts to provide principles in terms of which the attainment of objectivity is to be construed. The criteria of objectivity are to be found in such notions as decentration and reversibility. Nevertheless the satisfaction of conditions such as that decentration must have taken place (and how does one decide that it has?) and that the structure of thought manifests reversibility can at best amount to the satisfaction of necessary conditions for the attainment of objectivity, not sufficient conditions. The parallel claim made by Kant is that the conformity of judgment to certain principles is a necessary condition of their being true for all men and not just for me; conformity to those principles might, on that thesis, distinguish judgment that claims to be objective from what may be merely a figment of the imagination (and

Hume left the matter just there with no means of making the distinction, so that no rational justification could be given for belief in an objective world). The function of Kant's argument is thus to show that I must make room for a distinction between what is due to me and what is not so due to me as a condition of both objectivity and subjectivity. Such an argument cannot, however, show anything about what will ensure that the distinction is given application; it can show only what else has to be the case *if* it is to be given application. One cannot by starting from features of one's own thought reach conclusions thereby about what must equally be so for others. The notion of objectivity, however, implies just that; it is not identical, by any means, with what is agreed by others, but it implies at least the possibility of being agreed by others.

It is this feature that is missing from Piaget's thinking about objectivity. It might be suggested that the notion of decentration at least implies a turning away from subjectivity in that it is the reverse of egocentricity. That it does that is true, but that fact implies only that we must find room for a distinction between what is due to or concerned with the self and what is not. It does not indicate how that distinction is to be given application. The notion of reversibility is not sufficient to provide the basis for the application of the distinction. To say that a form of thought involves reversibility is in effect to imply that it has a degree of logical sophistication, coherence and rationality. However admirable it may be in many ways that a form of thought should have such qualities, they do not ensure that the form of thought is objective; what one thinks can be extremely logical without thereby being in the running for truth. It is not even enough to say, as Piaget does, that the construction of reality presupposes 'a constant reference to experiences'. That is not so merely for the *ad hominem* reason that Piaget's account of perception as distorting unless modified by intelligence scarcely provides any kind of independent foundation for thought. It is also that we need some assurance that the experiences in question are veridical; i.e., we need a criterion for the distinction between veridical and non-veridical experiences.

The point could be put in another way by asking how the notion of knowledge fits into the kinds of model that Piaget uses to explain cognitive development. (It is at this point, in connection with knowledge, that the whole notion of cognitive development becomes most problematic.)[12] In adopting his biological approach Piaget often uses terms such as 'biological knowledge', but the justification for the use of such terms rests only on the general analogy that he sees between cognitive development and more general biological development. The acceptability of that analogy itself, however, turns on whether the concept of knowledge can be construed in strict biological terms; hence, unless further considerations were adduced the argument would be circular. It might be argued that the further considerations lie in the detailed working out of the analogy that Piaget provides in *Biology and Knowledge*; but in fact that working out is merely a detailed extension of the analogy and does not bring forward independent considerations. The idea that the cognitive development of the individual can be seen as a sequential succession of equilibrations brought about through assimilation and accommodation is at least commensurate with the idea that it can also be seen as a progressive structuring of the world by the individual. All that is lacking in the second idea to make it strictly commensurate with the first is the idea that the structuring must follow certain necessary paths if it is to result in the mature way of structuring things. A mature way of structuring things, however, is not *eo ipso* the *right* way of structuring things; yet it should be this if it is to be knowledge.

To structure things is to classify and relate them. Provided that one classifies things as such and suches and relates them on certain principles, classifying and relating can be said to be the other side of the coin from having concepts. That is to say that to classify something as a such and such one must have the concept of the such and such in question; and to have the latter one must be in the position to classify things accordingly. Thus having the concept of X involves a knowledge of the principles of classification that apply to Xs, provided, if it is to be knowledge, that those principles are objective. That proviso is extremely important. To put ships and shoes and sealing-wax, cabbages and kings together is not to follow any obvious principle of classification (unless one invokes the sounds that the words make when spoken); but putting them together is a way of structuring the world in one sense of those words. If the decision to put them together is not a totally arbitrary one, it can be said that the person concerned believes that they fall together and believes that they are all such and suches, whatever 'such and such' may be. Thus it can be seen that one way of structuring the world is correlative with and can be explained in terms of believing things to be such and suches and thus of a kind. It does not, however, amount to knowledge, since, among other things, we have no assurance that the way of structuring the world is an objective one. (For reasons that I shall come to later, I do not think that even this is enough.

since I do not think that one can have beliefs without having knowledge in some way.) If, then, to have the concept of X is to know what it is for things to be X, and thus to know the principles of classification for Xs, it is impossible to give a sufficient explanation of what it is to have and acquire concepts in terms of the notion of structuring alone.

This is not in itself to deny that in the development of the individual there may come into being complex structures and structural relationships both within the individual's nervous system and between it and the environment. It may equally be true that if these structures are to come into being various sub-structures will have to come into being first, so that the system considered as such will have to pass through various stages. The necessity for this, however, will depend on its being the kind of system that it is and will hold only in relation to the end to be attained. All this could feasibly be construed in biological terms. That alone, however, would not justify our speaking of *knowledge* in this connection; nor would it alone justify the claim that in order to have certain forms of knowledge one must of necessity pass through other stages of knowledge in a given order. On the other hand, if, as I said earlier, we approach the matter from the side of knowledge, then, while there are undoubtedly cases in which one can say that one cannot know A without knowing B, this does not entail that one must first know B and then A, let alone that the temporal ordering of the acquisition of knowledge must always be a linear one. Hence there is no necessary fit between the story about structures and the story about the implications of the concept of knowledge for the interrelationships between items of knowledge. If it seems plausible to say that concrete knowledge must precede abstract knowledge,[13] the reverse conception is not self-contradictory; it is merely something that we should find unintelligible in general in relation to our conception of a normal human being.[14] A contingent course of development, over which no claims to necessity could be made, is of course quite another matter; if it is a fact that people acquire knowledge in certain ways and in a certain general order, then it is a fact, and we should seek to understand why it is so, even if it is open to us to ask whether there are any conditions under which the facts might be otherwise.

The acquisition of knowledge, however, is in effect the initiation into a body of knowledge that others either share or might in principle share. This is because the standards of what counts as knowledge (and, since knowledge implies truth, the standards of what counts as true also) are interpersonal. The concepts of knowledge, truth and objectivity are social in the sense that they imply a framework of agreement on what counts as known, true and objective.[15] It is not that what is true, etc. is what society determines as such. To suppose *that* is to commit a fallacy which runs through a good deal of the so-called sociology of knowledge; there may well be a viable sociology of beliefs, but not, properly speaking, a sociology of knowledge. Nevertheless, if something is claimed as knowledge it must be possible in principle to show that it is so by following recognised procedures, or something of the kind, whether or not the person making the claim can himself go through these moves. All this implies a context in which others come into the picture in such a way that agreement with them is not only a general possibility but presupposed at certain points. It is for this reason that the epistemological approach which starts from the position of the individual alone set against the rest of the world is so wrong. The fact that such an approach fits in with the biological approach which similarly considers the individual organism in relation to its environment equally shows the inappropriateness of that as a model on which to construe the growth of knowledge and cognitive development generally.

When, therefore, it is said that Piaget seriously underestimates the social in his approach, it is not just that he underestimates the efficacy of social factors in producing deviations from the normal pattern of development which he thinks necessary for the reasons given; it is also that he ignores the necessity of bringing others into the picture as part of the context in which alone the concept of knowledge can get a purchase. Thus a purely biological model and the epistemological approach which is commensurate with it must prove inadequate for the task in hand. Adding structure to genesis ensures that the growth of knowledge and understanding is not simply thought of as contingent on the way in which experience falls, as it is with empiricism. Adding genesis to structure ensures that knowledge and understanding are at least thought of as developing in some sense. The idea of genesis with structure, however, does not explain why it is that what develops in this way without being subject simply to the vagaries of experience is in fact knowledge. It is clear that we need to broaden the terms of reference for the discussion of our problem.

I have already referred to the necessity of bringing in other people. I think that it is also important that what we should be concerned with in this context is *people*, not just organisms, epistemic subjects, would-be scientists, theory constructors, and the other *personae* that have figured in my discussion so far. To put the matter in another way, a proper account of the conditions necessary for the growth of understanding and knowledge in the individual in the face of experience depends upon a full recognition of what human beings are and of what a human form of life is. The working out of some of the details of this will be my task in the next few chapters. One point ought perhaps to be made at this stage. In the Introduction I made some remarks about the question why the problems with which I am concerned should be considered to be philosophical problems. Some of those with whom I have been concerned in the interval would consider themselves primarily as psychologists. That fact provokes again the question why the story that I am about to try to tell is not one that belongs to psychology. Even if I am not concerned with the empirical details, I shall be concerned, it might be said, with the general theory into which those details would have to fit. Am I not therefore attempting to produce a psychological theory *a priori?* Some might object to the departmental or compartmental basis on which the question is raised; surely people with different training and different competences might nevertheless make contributions towards the solution of a single problem. Whatever might be said on that theme —and I am not entirely convinced of it—I believe that what I shall be concerned with is philosophical all the same. My aim is to provide some kind of understanding of the concepts in terms of which any adequate theory of the growth of knowledge and understanding through experience should be worked out. I shall not try to provide that theory but to provide an understanding of the conceptual framework within which an adequate theory would find a purchase. I believe that both philosophers and psychologists have too often ignored or failed to notice all that is essential to that framework.

In the account that I shall offer I shall not attempt to start from the beginning of the child's intellectual development and work forwards in a linear way. Rather, I shall first try to say something about the general nature of experience and its relations to knowledge and understanding, and only then go on to say something about its presuppositions and the terms in which we are to understand how that knowledge and understanding arise in the child.

Experience and understanding: 5
I Perception

I noted in chapter 2 that Aristotle uses the term 'experience' (*empeiria*) to refer to a form of knowledge which is less than scientific knowledge proper, in that it is dependent upon the repetition of sense-impressions combined with memory, and has a primary concern with particulars rather than universals. I do not intend to review yet again the account that Aristotle offers of the genesis of experience and knowledge; it is with the nature of experience that I am now concerned. I noted previously that the sense of the term 'experience', as Aristotle uses it, is roughly that which we presuppose when we say that our experience of someone is that he is such and such or refer to a man of experience. If we speak of knowledge being founded on experience we mean something similar; we mean to speak of what we find out by the use of our senses. It may well be the case that the elements that Aristotle mentions in his account of the genesis of experience are to be mentioned in any adequate account of what experience is. In that case experience would involve sense-perception, memory and the recognition of their objects as particulars of certain kinds.

These same elements are to be found in Kant's account of experience in the so-called 'Threefold Synthesis' in that part of his *Critique of Pure Reason* concerned with the Transcendental Deduction of the Categories. For Kant experience of an object is not just a function of sense or sensibility; it requires the use of the understanding helped by the imagination. Through this the manifold of experiences that we are presented with in perception is synthesised, and the synthesis has to take place in three ways. First, a bundle or collection of appearances with which we are furnished in sense-perception has to be taken together as a unity (Kant calls this the 'synthesis of apprehension', the experiences that we receive in looking at, say, a house are taken together and not in a discrete way). Second, the appearances of an object over a period of time have also to be taken together as a unity so that the bundle has an identity through time (Kant calls this the 'synthesis of reproduction', since it depends on memory). Third, the appearances which constitute the bundle so specified have all to be taken as appearances of the same thing, so falling under a specific concept which provides their final principle of unity (Kant calls this the 'synthesis of recognition', the experiences that we receive in looking at a house are taken as experiences *of* something, ideally of course as experiences of a house).

We need not here go further into or attempt to assess Kant's account in detail. It does, however, seem plausible to suppose that experience of objects does involve at least the three things mentioned: sense-experiences, memory to the extent of making possible awareness of identity through time, and concepts. Experiences of a thing will then be knowledge of something having identity in space and time as an instance of a certain kind of thing, under the condition that this is mediated through sense-experiences. Such a form of knowledge will presuppose other knowledge, since it will presuppose the knowledge of what it is for a thing to possess an identity through space and time, and, even more pertinently, the knowledge of what it is for a thing to be an instance of a given kind—knowledge which is involved in having the concept in question. Both these forms of knowledge, however, are in a sense general, while the knowledge of the object as an instance of what is so known is knowledge of a particular. It is the mediation of sense-experiences which makes possible in this case the application of the general knowledge to the particular. To say this, however, is to do little more than state the problem; for it is what the mediation consists in that turns out to be so puzzling. It is so puzzling in fact that some philosophers have tried to do without it altogether, or have at least tried to explain the idea of having a sense-experience in terms of belief or knowledge. Such a view thus incorporates the idea that perception can be elucidated in terms of belief and knowledge alone.

One striking example of this kind of view is that put forward by D.M. Armstrong in his *Perception and the Physical World* and repeated with modifications in his *Materialist Theory of the Mind.* The view fits in well with a materialist point of view that is opposed to dualism; experiences such as sensations have seemed to many the chief obstacle to a rejection of dualism. The view that perception can be elucidated entirely in terms of belief or knowledge involves a rejection of what has been called, in the case of visual perception, 'non-epistemic seeing', a form of seeing that entails no beliefs or knowledge on the part of the perceiver about the object of his perception. It should be noted that an acceptance of non-epistemic seeing involves only the thesis that some forms of perception cannot be exhaustively elucidated in terms of knowledge or belief; it is another matter to go further and claim that such forms of perception, and perhaps all, also involve having sensations or sense-experiences of that kind. One philosopher who has made much use of the notion of non-epistemic seeing is Fred Dretske in his book *Seeing and Knowing*. Dretske's reason for invoking the notion is that he thinks that without it there would be no point of focus for our beliefs in such a way that those beliefs might have the common and public basis that is ultimately required for sense-perception. In this way and for this reason he takes non-epistemic seeing to be a form of visual discrimination *simpliciter*. For reasons that will appear later I think that he is wrong to look for non-epistemic seeing at this level and for this purpose, but the notion has in any case a wider application than that.

It is not to be denied, of course, that some perception does involve belief or knowledge: that is to say, taking sight as our prototype for perception in general, there is epistemic seeing in the sense that when we see that such and such, or sometimes when we see something as such and such, we *ipso facto* believe or know something, or come to believe or know something. Some seeing, one might put it, is believing. If this were not so one might justifiably wonder what the point of having senses might be. One would be left perhaps with the possibility of a merely aesthetic attitude to the world, but it is difficult to see how even this idea could gain a purchase unless perception also provided us with the means of distinguishing things as suitable objects for aesthetic attitudes. That would undoubtedly involve beliefs that the objects were of that kind. It seems plausible to suggest, therefore, that non-epistemic forms of perception are parasitical upon epistemic forms. It is only because we are capable of having perceptual beliefs that we can speak in our case of non-epistemic *perception*. A creature which could not come to have beliefs in the course of perception would be a purely sensory creature, one which might have sensations but not perception at all properly speaking.

To say this is to presuppose a distinction between sensation and perception, a distinction which has not really figured in my discussion so far. In discussing Aristotle and Kant I spoke of sense-experiences or sense-impressions, a way of speaking which leaves it ambiguous whether it is sensation or perception with which we are concerned. I did this because the philosophers in question spoke in that way, so that an ambiguity exists in their thinking and writing on these matters, as it has done in the great majority of thinkers in this area.[1] Thomas Reid, the eighteenth-century Scottish philosopher, who deserves, in my opinion, more attention that he normally gets for maintaining the distinction in a clear and systematic way, defined a sensation as an act of mind which 'hath no object distinct from the act itself'.[2] Whatever may be thought of this definition, particularly the reference to an *act* of mind, there is much to be said for the idea that a sensation is such that in having it we are conscious of it and not of anything else, except incidentally. The qualification is necessary because in, for example, having a pain caused by some object external to the body we may incidentally be aware also of that object or some of its properties. It may also be necessary to make another qualification in that we sometimes speak of having had a pain over a certain period of time but only being conscious or aware of it from time to time when our attention was not distracted or turned to other things. If all perception involves having sensations, it is not generally the case that in perceiving an object we are aware of the sensations produced by that object, as opposed to the object itself; thus the sensations will have to be like the pain which we are not aware of because we are not paying attention to it, and for the same reasons. I shall return to this point later. It remains true that to the extent that we are conscious of our sensations it is them that we are conscious of in having them and not anything else, except incidentally.

Reid goes on to say that perception can be distinguished from sensation by the fact that it possesses three other characteristics, i.e. three characteristics other than the the incidence of a sensation. He says that for perception there is also required (1) 'A conception or notion of the object perceived', (2) 'a strong and irresistible conviction and belief of its present existence', and (3) an immediacy in this belief such that it is not the result of reasoning.[3] I think that he is right about the necessity for a concept, in the sense that we cannot properly be said to see something unless we see it *as* something or other, even if we do not see it as it is. On the other hand, the references to the necessity for a belief seems wrong, even though he restricts the belief in question to one in the existence of the object. We do not believe in the existence of everything that we take ourselves to see, and even when we do have beliefs in perceiving things those beliefs are not necessarily immediate in the sense that Reid specifies. Beliefs about the size or distance of a perceived object, for example, may indeed involve inference on some occasions, although not on all. Thus while Reid seems right to make a distinction between sensation and perception, he is not entirely right in what he says about each. In particular, perception does not always involve belief, at any rate not in any straight-forward way.

On the other hand, Reid seems right about the place of concepts in perception, although it is necessary to be careful in stating the point. It has sometimes been said that all seeing is seeing-as, all perception perceiving-as, and as a slogan this has much to recommend it. If we are to see something we must see it as something or other; we must, that is, see it under some description, under some concept. The words 'as something or other' need to be emphasised however. If we are to see something we do not have to see it as it actually is. There is indeed a use of 'see as' such that it is even permissible to say of someone that he saw X even if that person had no idea of what an X is. The point may be put technically by saying that the description under which he saw whatever he saw may be only extensionally related to the description under which the object properly falls; there is no necessary connection between the two descriptions such that it would follow that if he saw it under one description it must be true that he saw it under the other. Someone who had no experience or knowledge of the trappings of civilisation might still quite properly be said to have seen a car even if he had no idea of what a car is and regarded it perhaps as magic or ju-ju. On the other hand, someone who had no idea of *anything* could not be said to see at all, and one who had no idea of anything relevant to the thing in question could not properly be said to see *it*—granted however that relevance is an extremely relative notion. The mere physiological functioning of the eyes is not enough to ensure that the ascription of visual perception is justified; nor is the having of experiences enough except with considerable qualifications on what is meant by 'experiences'. If perception, then, necessarily involves the having of concepts—if, that is, perception necessarily involves an understanding or knowledge of at least something about the world—it must be wrong to invoke a notion of non-epistemic seeing which excludes having concepts as one of its conditions. Such seeing would not be *seeing*. Dretske, as I have already noted, speaks of non-epistemic seeing as mere visual discrimination, or rather he uses the notion in such a way as to confine it to that; but even discrimination must involve discriminating things as such and suches, or at least as different.

The fact that perception presupposes the having of concepts does not entail, however, that perception is analysable purely in terms of belief or knowledge. What I have said so far implies that perception involves belief and knowledge only to the extent that it presupposes concepts, given that having a concept implies understanding and therefore knowledge on the part of the perceiver. From the fact that to perceive X we must perceive it as something and to that extent know or understand what it is for a thing to be a something of that kind, it does not follow that the perception of X is totally explicable in terms of belief or knowledge about X. Nor does it follow that it is enough to say that when we perceive something it is simply the case that we know or believe something because of the way in which our sense-organs and our nervous system have been stimulated. It is not enough, that is, in giving an account of what perception is, to add to the statement that the perceiver has knowledge or belief about the object of perception an account of how that knowledge or belief is produced, by reference to facts about the stimulation of the sense-organs and nervous system. That it is *not* enough can be seen from two sorts of consideration. First, as I have already suggested but must now do more to show, there are cases of perception in which how we perceive things is not a function of knowledge or beliefs that we have. Second, if there were cases of someone coming to have knowledge or belief *merely* as a result of the stimulation of his nervous system there would still be reason *not* to call this sense-perception. I shall take each of these considerations in turn.

The first consideration, that there are cases of perception in which how we see things is not a function of knowledge or beliefs that we have, has been well set out by others. It is a primary feature of Dretske's book, even if he is not right to use non-epistemic seeing as a basis on which is to be constructed all those cases in which perception does involve beliefs about the object or objects in question. It is also a central feature of Roderick Chisholm's *Perceiving*, to the extent that he isolates a sense of the word 'appear' which is non-epistemic, in that to say of something that it appears such and such in this sense of the word 'appears' is not to attribute beliefs to the person to whom it so appears. The sun appears, looks or seems bigger at the horizon than at the zenith; but to say this is not necessarily to suggest anything about the beliefs of those to whom it so appears, let alone anything about what they know. I might mention finally what seems to me (i.e. what I believe to be—this use of 'seems' *is* epistemic) an excellent criticism of Armstrong's views, combined with an exposition of a passage from Aristotle which may well make the same point, by K. Lycos in an article entitled 'Aristotle and Plato on Appearing' in *Mind*, 1964.[4]

The point at issue can perhaps be most clearly illuminated by reference to those perceptual illusions which can be classified as 'sensory' (the zenith-horizon illusion referred to above is probably a case in point, and so is the Müller-Lyer illusion referred to in discussing Piaget). There are some illusions that are to be explained by reference to things that the perceiver believes or knows; it is said, for example, that a belief in the extreme importance of an object for the perceiver may make it look to him bigger in size than it normally does to others. Equally there are some illusions that cannot be explained in that way. However the Müller-Lyer illusion, for example, is to be explained, it does not seem to be explicable by reference to the beliefs of the perceiver, or at any rate not entirely so. The illusion is not normally affected by what one knows about the lengths of the lines with the arrow-heads attached to them. Even if one knows quite well that the lines are of the same length they will normally still look different in length. It is true that one *can* make them look the same length by, for example, diverting one's attention from the arrow-heads at their ends, but one cannot do it by simply dwelling on what one in fact knows about them: that they are of the same length. (It has been claimed by Richard Gregory in *Eye and Brain* that the illusion is due to experience of three-dimensional objects, in that we see the lines as if they are the corners of rooms or the external angles of buildings; but it is far from clear that we do have any tendency to see the lines in a three-dimensional way, as would be necessary for this account to hold good.)

One might also in this context refer to the fact, noted in the last chapter, that according to Piaget and his associates, as reported in *The Mechanisms of Perception*, illusions of this kind are at their extreme, in the sense that they manifest themselves to the largest extent, when experience and therefore presumably knowledge are at their minimum. They are at their extreme, Piaget claims, at an early age, and even if they never disappear completely they diminish as the child grows. The crucial point here, if the findings are correct (and I do not know of any reason for doubting them), is that the illusions are at their maximum at an age when beliefs about, for example, the length of the lines in the Müller-Lyer illusion must surely be at their minimum. If that is so, then the way things look and how we see them must sometimes be a function of something other than our beliefs, a function perhaps of the ways in which our experiences are brought about by features of the objects perceived.

The second consideration that I mentioned earlier is in fact connected with this same point. What seems to be missing from any account of perception and how things look which tries to explain or analyse perception entirely in terms of beliefs or knowledge is any reference to experiences. It is reasonable to protest, against such a view, that how things look is a *phenomenal* matter, and that to say this is to say something about the way in which experiences figure in our perception of them. We might imagine a creature which comes to have beliefs when its body is stimulated in ways that are characteristic of the ways in which sense-organs are stimulated in ordinary perception, but in the case of which there seems no question of its having experiences. We might suppose that except for that last point the creature is in all respects like us (although in saying this, of course, I might well be accused of begging the question, since what determines whether it is having experiences is one of the crucial points at issue). I doubt whether in fact such a science-fiction conception would be coherent in the long run in any case, but my concern in the present context is merely with the question of its coherence at the local level of whether the conception would be sufficient to provide a backing for an adequate account of ordinary human perception. It seems to me that without experiences such a creature could have no idea of how things look in any sense that made no reference to what it believed. While, for example, the pattern of light coming from the arrows on the lines in the Müller-Lyer illusion might cause the creature, on the supposition in question, to have beliefs about the lengths of the lines, it could never be in the position to have any idea of how the lines look independently of any beliefs of that kind, let alone in contrast with those beliefs, as may be the case with ordinary human perceivers.

It has sometimes been suggested, perhaps to meet a point of this kind, that even if we do not in fact believe that the lines in the illusion are of different length we may nevertheless have an inclination or disposition so to believe. I do not think that this is so in any sense that prevents the notions of an inclination or a disposition from becoming empty. For my own part I think that it is true to say that I have no such inclination in the circumstances in question, and I can see no reason why it should be supposed that there must be an inclination or disposition of this kind in any positive senses of those words. Sometimes, to obviate the point at issue, a lesser claim has been made in this context: that we should say or believe that the lines were of different length did we not know to the contrary. That claim may well be correct so far as it goes, but it does not meet the case; for it will hardly do as an account of what it *means to say* that the lines look of different length. Apart from any other considerations, if asked why we should say or believe that the lines were of different length did we not know to the contrary, we should surely have to say that it is because that is how they look. It is the look of the lines that explains our inclination or disposition to believe, if we have anything of that kind, and also explains the fact that we should so believe if we did not know otherwise; the facts in question cannot therefore be offered as an account of what 'looks' means in this context. The creature that I postulated, on the other hand, could not *ex hypothesi* offer such an explanation, since, without the relevant experiences, the sense of 'look' which is in question could have no application for it. It follows that the creature is not an adequate model of a human being in the respects that concern us. Sensory experiences, which fall under the concept of perception, thus seem to be in some way a condition of perception. (The above argument may well not seem conclusive. That there are cases of non-epistemic seeing and non-epistemic appearing seems clear; that this implies that perception presupposes something that falls under the concept of sensation is not so clear. Apart from the amplification of the point that follows, however, I do not know what further can be supplied by way of argument.)

It may be as well to put these points into relation with the other points about non-epistemic seeing that I made earlier. I said then that it was wrong to suggest that non-epistemic seeing could be made the foundation of epistemic seeing, and I suggested that in fact the concept of non-epistemic seeing is in a sense parasitical on that of epistemic seeing. How is it that I can now say that perception, which includes epistemic seeing, is dependent upon sensory experiences which fall under the concept of sensation? Is not non-epistemic seeing very close to sensory experience in that sense? The answer is that in fact the two concepts of non-epistemic seeing and sensory experience are very different, even if Dretske goes some of the way towards assimilating them in claiming that non-epistemic seeing can be elucidated in terms of mere visual differentiation. To say of a creature that it is having sensory experiences, where these are equivalent to sensations, is not *ipso facto* to say that it is perceiving anything. That is clear enough in the case of the bodily senses, where having a particular sensation can be seen to conform to Reid's criterion, to the extent that it need involve no consciousness of anything beyond it. Indeed, if we come to have knowledge or beliefs about an object via the sensation which is caused by it this is likely to be because we have further knowledge of what sort of object characteristically produces a sensation of that kind. Normally, however, the perception of an object is not a matter of inference from the properties of a sensation; rather, the sensation is a causal condition, and not a sufficient condition at that, for the perception. How a thing looks in the non-epistemic sense may be the basis for an inference to the real nature or characteristics of the thing, but non-epistemic seeing cannot be merely a causal condition of epistemic seeing, let alone a causal condition of seeing in general; and similarly for other forms of perception apart from seeing.

There has sometimes been scepticism on whether it is possible to isolate anything like a sensation in the case of all forms of perception or perhaps even in any. I have rehearsed arguments on the issue, with particular reference to Gilbert Ryle's position on it, elsewhere, particularly in my *Sensation and Perception* (ch. 11). I shall not repeat all the arguments here. Apart from the general considerations about the relation of perception to sensory experience which I have already surveyed, it is perhaps worth mentioning the following. The notion of sensation gets its clearest application in the case of bodily feelings such as pains, so much so that many people take what holds good of this paradigm application of the concept as exhausting the concept itself. Thus an objection that is often made to the thesis that forms of perception such as vision involve or presuppose having sensations is 'Do you mean sensations such as irritations in the eyes?' It is clear, however, that in the case of some forms of perception a definite distinction can be made between the perception and the sensations that this involves. Thus when we run our finger tips over an object with a certain texture, say a fabric, we may have tingling sensations in our fingers. In some cases of this kind, although not perhaps all, we may by this means feel the texture that the object has. In the latter case we are having a form of perception. It is often easy enough for us to switch our attention from the properties of the object felt to the sensations that we are having in our fingers. Of course, to claim that when we perceive by touch the texture of an object we are *ipso facto* having sensations in our fingers, even when we are not attending to them, is to suppose that we may have sensations without really being aware of them directly. Some may find this objectionable; but it seems to me but one more extension of the point that I made when introducing my discussion of the concept of sensation, that we may sometimes want to speak of having a sensation despite the fact that because our attention is elsewhere we are not directly aware of it.

My view is that what obviously holds good of touch is extendible to the other senses, although it is more natural to make this move in the case of some of the senses than in the case of others. For a keen analyst there may be scope for speaking of auditory sensations in connection with certain musical sonorities. It is perhaps rarely if ever pertinent to speak of visual sensations. The fact that it is not ordinarily pertinent so to speak, however, is not an overriding reason for refusing, in the course of a philosophical treatment of perception, to allow a place for sensations in the case of forms of perception such as vision if the general line of argument seems to demand that we do so allow it. Sensations associated with vision will not be exactly like sensations associated with touch, but that is no objection. (It has to be said, however, that there are certain technical difficulties in the case of vision over the individuation of sensations, over what marks one off from another. There are not available in this case such considerations as bodily location, and since by 'sensation' I do not mean anything like 'sense-datum' one cannot distinguish sensations by their objects; for they have none in the way that a sense-datum can be said to be, if one chooses so to talk, *of* red. See the further arguments in my paper 'The Visual Field and Perception')

It seems to me, therefore, that there are good reasons in general for supposing that the having of sensations is a condition of perception taking place, and that the type of condition is a causal one.[5] Sense-perception requires the having of sense-experiences or sensations as its causal condition, but it goes beyond these in involving also consciousness of an independent object and consciousness of it as a such and such. Thus, if perception is to be attributed to something, that something must be conscious in such a way that it has sensory experiences under certain specific conditions connected with the stimulation of its sense-organs in appropriate ways. It must also be capable of what Brentano called 'intentionality', or consciousness of objects in the formal sense of 'object' which does not commit one on the question whether anything of that kind actually exists; it must have, as one might put it, consciousness *of*. It must also have an understanding of what a range of specific non-formal objects consist in; it must, that is, have the concepts under which a range of possible objects of perception fall. These separate conditions, however, are somehow united in the perception so that the perceiver sees objects as such and suches; he sees whatever is the object of perception as falling under a concept or concepts under the conditions that the sensory experiences provide in making the perception in question *sense*-perception. For it is conceptually possible that there should be forms of consciousness of objects as such and suches which are not, as one might put it, sense-consciousness, not sense-perception. The satisfaction of the condition that there are sense-experiences brings with it the satisfaction of the condition that these are due in turn to the causal conditions appropriate to sense-perception; otherwise it would not be sense-perception, but, say clairvoyance.

71

Furthermore, if, as I think and have already suggested, having a concept of X is knowing what it is for something to be an X (something that admits of degrees, since one might know this to some extent or in some part only), it follows that perceiving something involves applying knowledge to particular cases. The having of sense-experiences which are themselves the product of a causal chain constitutes a causal condition which makes possible this application of knowledge to particular cases. The growth of experience is in this sense a growth of knowledge in application to cases under these conditions. It implies both understanding of some kind on the part of the person concerned and suitable conditions under which that understanding may have application to cases; it is sense-perception which supplies the latter. A man of experience is one who has been enabled to develop understanding of a range of matters in application to cases. Something cannot, however, be seen as a case without prior understanding of some kind on the part of the person concerned, and that is why it may sometimes be of no use to present a person with a certain range of experience as an educational process. He has to be able to make sense of it; the objects in question have to be objects that he can perceive as such and in such a way as is relevant to the educational process in question. The person has to be in a position to make use of the experience if knowledge and further understanding are to emerge from it; and that implies prior understanding of some kind or other. Perception and experience thus logically imply understanding in the sense that they *presuppose* understanding of some kind (although they need not presuppose it temporally). At the same time they may provide the foundation for the growth of further understanding. The development of understanding on the basis of prior understanding may come about through the connection of one concept with others in various ways, and through a kind of interplay between concepts and instances or cases that perception and its conditions make possible.

It should be clear that this process cannot be of the kind that I indicated in chapter 2 when discussing a possible interpretation of Aristotle's genetic account, the one that makes the growth of experience simply dependent on repetition at each previous stage. For that account (at any rate if not supplemented by the teaching/ learning function of induction) makes the process totally causal, as does any account based on conditioning. Given the story that I have presented about the way in which perception comes about and the way in which it figures in experience itself, such accounts may be seen to be insufficient and it may also be seen why this is so. The growth of experience is something that takes place under causal conditions but it is not totally causal. To see that fully, and how it is so, the issues must now be approached from the side of concepts and the part that they play in perception and experience. All that I have said about that so far is that a condition of properly being said to perceive is that one must have concepts. Concepts cannot, therefore, be all derived *from* perception since some concepts are presupposed in perception. One cannot be said to perceive at all unless and until one understands *something* of those things which stand as objects to perception. How then does this understanding come about and how much of it is presupposed?

Before I turn to this question, however, let me make one *caveat* on what I have said about perception. In saying what I have so far said I have been concerned solely with the necessary conditions of perception and thereby of experience. I have said little or nothing about how those conditions fit together. It is possible to understand why it is plausible to say, as Aristotle does, that perception and experience involve a concern with particulars; for while it is not true to say that they have no concern with universals (one can see beauty or misery in the world, for example), seeing the universal or general characteristics is something that depends on the satisfaction of particular conditions and takes place on particular occasions in particular circumstances. When those conditions are satisfied, then, provided that one has the relevant knowledge of what it is for something to be an X, one may have that form of consciousness of an object that we call perceiving it as X. It is possible to be aware or conscious of an object as X without perceiving it as X, and one can attempt to set out, as I have done, what else has to be satisfied if that awareness is to be a perceptual awareness. That, however, does not make the perceptual awareness itself any the less puzzling. It is one of those phenomena that are so ordinary that, as Wittgenstein put it, we do not find it puzzling enough. Wittgenstein's discussion of 'seeing-as' in *Philosophical Investigations* (II, xi) is concerned in large part with those perceptual experiences in which the look of a thing may be changed by something like the use of the imagination. There are also those experiences when the look of a thing may be changed completely by the sudden recognition of what it is or of what sort of thing it is. There are again the expereinces when the look of a thing may be changed by a sudden alteration in the causal conditions. It is easy enough to say something about the circumstances in which this sort of thing happens, but that does not make the experience itself any less puzzling and difficult to spell out. I shall leave the matter there, having indicated the puzzlement and its source.[6]

6 Experience and understanding: II Concepts and their conditions

I have said more than once already that, as I understand the matter, to have the concept of X is to know what it is for something to be X, and that this can be a matter of degree since one can have knowledge of some aspects of X without necessarily knowing others. To have *a* concept of X is to believe something about what it is for something to be X, and this belief may or may not be right. To the extent that we can speak of the correct or right understanding of something, we can speak of *the* concept of that thing, and *the* concept is therefore objective and shareable with others. Belief presupposes knowledge to the extent that one must know what it is that one is believing about and what it is for something to be what that thing is believed to be.[1] Thus it seems to follow that one cannot have *a* concept of something unless one has *the* concept of something or other (though not necessarily of that of which one has *a* concept). A subjective understanding presupposes participation in a public and objective understanding at some point; it is in this sense that it presupposes knowledge. Thus my claim that perception involves having concepts entails that perception presupposes knowledge in a logical, though not necessarily temporal, sense of 'presuppose'. Something cannot properly be said to see X unless it has knowledge of something in terms of which X is seen (though that knowledge does not have to be knowledge of X as such). That does not, however, entail that the knowledge has to precede the perception in time; they may, for example, come together. Nevertheless it does entail that a creature cannot properly be said to perceive things unless it is capable of having relevant knowledge, and this applies to animals and infants (i.e. non-language-users), as well as to mature, adult human beings. I shall begin my consideration of concepts and their conditions by discussing the attribution of concepts to animals, as the case of animals raises certain issues in a particularly acute form; the considerations to be derived from this can then be applied to the case of infants and thereby to developmental issues generally.

Some philosophers have refused to attribute concepts to animals at all or have claimed that it is a 'courtesy attribution' only.[2] It is difficult to understand this last notion, unless it is a way of saying that it is not really an attribution at all. Certainly there are many concepts which it would make little sense to attribute to animals, except in a very attenuated form. I would therefore agree with Geach's strictures[3] on ascribing the concept of a triangle to rats on the basis of learning experiments in which the rats learn to jump at a door with a triangle on it rather than, say, a square. Whatever the rats see the pattern on the door *as*, it cannot illuminatingly be said that they see it as a triangle. Knowledge of what it is for something to be a triangle involves knowledge of geometry and geometrical properties, and what rats could know of the characteristics of pattern of this sort would not be enough to make it anything but misleading to say that they know anything of what a triangle is. Nevertheless, they clearly see the pattern as something, and the general trend of their behaviour may suggest that they see it as something which, in contradistinction to the other pattern, has *some* relevance to our ways of distinguishing the pattern. If that is so, what they know of the characteristics of the pattern in question must have *some* connection with what we as human beings know.

A general objection to such a conclusion might be made as follows. Geach brings forward in his *Mental Acts* a theory of concepts which makes them something 'presupposed to' judgment. For the most part Geach seems also to want to restrict concepts to language-users, or at least to those who have acquired the use of language whether or not they have subsequently lost it for some reason. I do not wish to tackle that view head on, although it seems to me in many ways mistaken. I wish rather to approach the matter through the thesis that concepts are presupposed to judgments, a view that seems to me in the main correct. To say that to have the concept of X is to know what it is for something to be X is to say also that it is to know *that* certain things are the case; it is to know that things of a certain general kind are Xs. If that is so, it follows that nothing could have a concept that could not form or make judgments. Once again this seems to me both correct and consistent with what Geach has to say. He maintains that the only plausible theory of judgment is an analogical one, according to which making a judgment is to be construed on the analogy of saying something. Geach's paradigm for this is the Biblical saying 'The fool hath said in his heart "There is no God" '. Saying in one's heart is judging. A similar thesis has been put forward by Bruce Aune in his *Knowledge, Mind and Nature*,[4] and it is once again a thesis that I have no wish to dispute. It might be taken to imply, however, that nothing could make judgments that did not know anything about sayings or propositions, and that the ability to make judgments is therefore restricted to language-users.

I think that it would be quite wrong to draw that conclusion. It has to be admitted that in attributing knowledge or judgments to non-language-users one has to express what they know or judge in terms that are intelligible to us and informative to us. It cannot be inferred from the fact that it is appropriate (or at any rate it seems so) to say of an animal that it believes that it is about to be fed that anything very like that proposition, i.e. a proposition expressed in those terms, passes through its mind. On the other hand, that is not in itself a reason for refusing to say that whatever it is that does pass through the animal's mind is properly expressible in propositional form and thus has, as one might put it, a propositional flavour. For a thought to be a genuine thought it must be about something, and something else must be thought about that something; so that there is in that thought something corresponding to the distinction between subject and predicate that becomes explicit in language itself. For this to be the case, there need not be in the actual expression of the thought for the thinker, whether internal of external, an *obvious* complexity of this kind. One might compare in this connection the claim made by the Russian psychologist, L. S. Vygostsky, that the first word spoken by a child amounts to a whole sentence.[5] Vygotsky's point is, in effect, that even if the speech of the child has no obvious grammatical or semantical complexity it is up for assessment as a saying. If so, the thought of which the word is an expression must be such that an appropriate description of it as far as we are concerned is that it is the thought that ... . There is indeed a general point to be made here about the aptness of descriptions of thought processes. I once heard R. K. Elliott suggest that a possible description of a baby's attitude to the satisfaction of its hunger might be that it was to the baby 'salvation and grace'. This suggestion produced a storm of protest to the effect that no baby could have such ideas. To my mind, however, the suggestion has an obvious plausibility and aptness. Nevertheless, the fact that this description may be an apt description of what passes through a child's mind by no means entails that we have to say that it was these thoughts *expressed in these ways* that passed through his mind.[6]

In a certain sense the same point, that there may be propositionally styled thought even when there is no language, can with some justification be attributed to Chomsky, although it is not his way of putting the matter. When Chomsky maintains that the learning of a particular language presupposes knowledge of the deep structure of language to which the surface structure of the actual language is linked, he can be construed as saying that the child knows some linguistic facts before he knows any actual language. Put in that way the thesis may sound odd and controversial. Since, however, one of the distinctions said to be present at the level of deep structure is that between subject and predicate, what is in effect being claimed, at any rate as far as that is concerned, is that the child, before learning any actual language, knows what it is for something to be *about* something else. If the matter is put in that way it is far from clear to me why it should be thought controversial.[7] *We* should describe the pre-linguistic child's thought in terms of the language of propositions, and we should be right to do so even if the child cannot make use of propositions in linguistic form. If this is correct, I take it that nothing prevents us from attributing judgments to the pre-linguistic child, at some stage of development at any rate, together with all that this entails. I mean by the latter some understanding, for example, of what it is for a thought to be right or wrong, something that at the propositional level amounts to the ideas of truth and falsity. I take it that the same also applies to animals, although I shall return to that matter and some further difficulties attached to it later.

Whatever may be said about pre-linguistic children, it is clear that there must be many restrictions on the possible understanding and concepts of animals, as I noted earlier. Charles Taylor has put the point in connection with what he calls the consciousness of animals by saying that we can attribute to animals only that consciousness which has immediate relevance to their behaviour; and he associates this with the point that human beings can see something as falling under a number of different descriptions, while an animal can see it only as it affects its immediate concerns.[8] The capacity possessed by human beings in this connection implies an ability to stand back from an object in a detached sort of way. Language is clearly of very great importance in this respect, since one thing that language makes possible is the provision of a focus for background knowledge and understanding which would otherwise have to be made explicit but which by its means can be left implicit. (See chapter 8 for a further elaboration of this point.) Even so, what Taylor says about animals may be too much of a generalisation; it may well be that some animals (e.g., chimpanzees) are capable to some extent of seeing some things in respects other than those which have immediate relevance to their behaviour. If chimpanzees can be taught some kind of use of signs,[9] they may also be able to see things under more than one description. When also, for example, Köhler's ape, Sultan, lighted upon the idea of fitting two sticks together to make a longer one in order to reach a banana, is it not feasible to say that he saw the sticks in more than one way?[10] However that may be, there seems no reason to refuse to attribute knowledge and understanding to animals together. It depends on the animal and the behaviour that it is capable of manifesting. Fish can swim, but we have no inclination to say that this involves knowledge, nor *should* we have such an inclination; but for animals that have learnt to do this it may be a very different story.

Locke's remark 'Brutes abstract not' is acceptable if it is taken to mean that animals cannot have the kind of second-order knowledge of an X which is presupposed in an ability to say what an X is. Knowledge of an X may, however, be a matter of degree, as I have previously said, and it may find application to cases in various ways. There is a sense in which someone may, for example, know what a clutch on a car is without being able to give any account of what it is, in that he is able to get into a car (one, of course, that does not have automatic transmission) and drive it away, using the clutch in the process. He knows what a clutch is in the sense that he can use it as part of the fairly complex skill involved in driving a car. One thing that makes driving a car a skill is that it involves some understanding of what one is doing, and since it is in part a manipulative skill some understanding also of what it is that one is operating with. A man who got into a car without automatic transmission and attempted to drive it away without using the clutch might in normal circumstances be justly accused of not knowing what a clutch is (although he might in some cases turn out, of course, to have a rather superior skill, since it *is* possible to drive without using the clutch). Moreover, there is even a sense in which being able to say what something is may be compatible with not knowing what it is in another way. By 'being able to say what something is' I do not mean merely being able to recite the appropriate formula, in the way that, for example, a student may in translating Virgil's *Georgics* may be able to say that *vicia* is vetch without having the slightest idea of what vetch is (an experience to which I was repeatedly subject in my days as a student of the classics). I am speaking of being able to say what something is in a way that reflects theoretical understanding, and my point is that this need not amount to full understanding of it. It would not necessarily affect what we said about the man who tried to drive a car which did not have automatic transmission without using the clutch if he was quite able to say what a clutch is if asked and even able to give a decent theoretical explanation of the workings of a clutch. Understanding what a clutch is in the full sense involves not only being able in principle to give an account of what it is but also being able in principle to recognise a clutch as an object for certain appropriate forms of behaviour. The complexities of the knowledge involved in this indicate how implausible it is to suppose that an account of what it is to have a concept can be provided in terms of a pattern of response to stimuli or in terms simply of the occurrence of a mental event. Even the suggestion that having a concept involves structuring things seems in this context rather thin, since the knowledge involved in having the concept is capable of manifestation in a variety of ways and cannot be achieved conceived in terms of any one way of structuring the world.

If all this is involved in having a concept in the full sense, it must be admitted that animals can never have concepts in the full sense. That, however, does not entail that they, or some of them, cannot be said to have concepts at all. Hence, if perception and experience presuppose concepts, animal forms of perception may be limited but not ruled out altogether.

We are apt, as I have already noted, to speak of animals (and equally of young children) in terms of the concepts that *we* possess. Thus we may say of a dog that runs around excitedly when its master (so-called) picks up its lead that it sees that it is going for a walk, even perhaps that it expects or hopes to do so.[11] If we say that the dog sees its master getting the lead we must not take this to imply, however, that the dog is thereby having attributed to it the concept of a master or that of a lead, or at least not in any significant sense. Such concepts bring with them complex forms of understanding, and in the case of the concept of a master at least there is presupposed an understanding of certain institutional relationships, which we should never have grounds for attributing to animals. The absence of language means that it is impossible for the animal to bring to bear at one time sufficient of the implications of the relationship without making them explicit; language, as I have said, provides a focus for the knowledge involved without its having to be made explicit (although it is less clear to me whether it is right to say that the animal cannot have the concept in question because it cannot use language, or whether it cannot have the use of language because it does not have sufficient of the kind of understanding in question). An animal might thus perhaps have an understanding of some of the elements that we suppose to be included in the concept of a master (e.g., perhaps an understanding of the fact that the human being has a certain power), without thereby being capable of understanding enough and in a sufficiently interrelated way to be said significantly to have the concept of a master. Once again, however, that does not prevent its being true that the dog sees what is happening under *some* concept or concepts. Indeed, it must do so if we are to attribute to it seeing at all; and it is more than doubtful whether our scepticism ought to stretch *that* far.

There is, however, another difficulty which the case of animal knowledge will serve to bring out, and which was implicit in what I said earlier about the thought of an animal or child having a propositional flavour. Perception, as we have seen, implies knowledge, at least in the sense that it implies knowledge of what it is for something to be whatever things are seen as. It is necessary to put the matter in that clumsy way, because while it is necessary, if something is to be seen, that it or its context be seen as something or other, it need not be seen for what it really is. However that may be, perception certainly implies knowledge in the sense that I have specified, although not necessarily in the sense that might usually be conveyed by saying 'Seeing is knowing'; seeing presupposes knowlege, it need not issue in further knowledge. The knowledge that *is* involved, however, is a knowledge of what it is for something to be such and such or knowledge *that* to be such and such is to be .... . Knowledge, of this kind at least, brings in its train the notion of truth. Someone cannot be said, or at least not properly said, to know that *p* if it is not true that *p*. More than this, however, while to know that *p* one need not be certain of the truth of *p* (for it is not necessary to know that one knows), one could not properly be said to know anything (any truth) if one had no idea of what truth is. (When I say 'knowledge of this kind', I make the qualification only to indicate that I am not here discussing other forms of knowledge, e.g., knowledge of, not to exclude the possibility that they too in the end bring in knowledge that.)

It has sometimes been claimed that the objects of knowledge and belief are different,[12] in that while the objects of belief may be propositions or some representation or expression of the facts, whether correct or incorrect, the object of knowledge is reality itself. There seems to me some truth in that claim; but it holds good only if 'object' is so construed as to be the object *for* the believer or knower respectively, i.e., in roughly the sense that Brentano was perhaps getting at in speaking of an intentional object. If I look out of the window, see that it is raining, and so form a belief to that effect, the object of my belief in the sense of *what my belief is about* is the state of affairs of the rain falling; the same applies to knowledge. In another sense, however, and the sense that I have been talking about, what I believe is *that* it is raining, and that may be said to be the object of my belief, whether or not my perception, and thus my belief, are correct. In order to have the belief I must have the conception of a representation or description of the facts, and that representation may or may not be correct. When I have knowledge I still know *that p*, so that if my perception of the rain amounts to knowledge I know *that* it is raining, but this description of the state of affairs is for me normally a description of the actual state of affairs, the facts. I say 'normally' to allow for those cases in which I may know something without knowing that I do. Such cases are, however, clearly derivative cases, and I could not properly be said to know something without knowing that I do if there were nothing that was a fact *for me* at all in the most obvious sense of 'for me'. In the cases in which we attribute knowledge although the person concerned does not know that he knows, we do so because, while the person in question is in the position for the facts to be facts for him, we think there is some reason why he will not look the facts in the face, so to speak. It seems to follow from all this that knowledge presupposes in the knower some conception of what it is for things to be so, a conception of reality or fact, and thus a conception of truth.

How does this get application in the case of animals? We must again be careful in interpreting the question. We need not imply that animals must be in the position to say what truth is (even philosophers have trouble with that!). But they must, if they are to have knowledge, be capable of standing in relation to truth in something of the way in which my driver stood in relation to a clutch. Just as he had to be capable of seeing it in some way as a clutch, with whatever that entails, so they must be capable of seeing things *as* true or false, or at least so or not so, and thus of seeing in some way the force of being right and wrong. The concept of truth, however, brings with it what Wittgenstein called 'agreement in judgments',[13] and in that sense (although in that sense only) the concept of truth is a social concept. It is not that the truth is simply what is agreed, but that there is a connection between what is true and what is agreed, in the sense that only in a context where it makes sense to speak of things being agreed and not agreed does it equally make sense to speak of truth. To say that is to say that the truth must in principle be public; a necessarily private truth makes no sense. To say the last is not to say that someone cannot know a truth which no one else knows is fact; it is to say that it would not be in place to speak of a truth which it is *logically impossible* for others to know. Thus to have a conception of truth is at least to have the idea of what is said to be true being a candidate for possible agreement by others; it is not something that one could have without the idea of possible agreement by and with others.

This is because, given the terms in which what is true is to be expressed, what is true and not true cannot be understood as such except within the framework of a public understanding. A conscious being that had no part in such a framework might, *as it were*, change its mind about something but could scarcely be said to have recognised thereby that what it had previously thought was false. Whether something is true or false is a question that gets application only in a public context. Hence it is difficult to see how something could acquire an understanding of what it is for things to be true and false outside that context. To the extent that we think that we can imagine something to which this does not apply we are nevertheless surreptitiously extending to it the framework which gives the suggestion intelligibility. Thus an animal may 'correct' its movements in a given situation (i.e. at least change them), but we can think of this as correction proper only to the extent that we can think of the animal as sharing *our* view of what is correct and incorrect, and thus sharing also *our* notions of correctness and incorrectness. With human beings this presents no problem, since with them there is no difficulty about giving application to the notions of agreement and disagreement. With *some* animals too the difficulties do not perhaps seem insuperable; for where learning and teaching go on the animal may be corrected and thus initiated into what is agreed and not agreed. For this to happen the animal must *eo ipso* be put in the way of seeing what it is to get something right or wrong. Even here, of course, the animal has to take correction *as* correction, and the problem of how this is possible applies both here and in the case of children; it is a problem to which I shall return later. What, however, of animals which have not been explicitly subjected to such correction and teaching?

When Wittgenstein speaks of the necessity for agreement in judgments as well as for, as he puts it, agreement in definitions, he does so in relation to the proviso 'if language is to be a means of communication'. It might be thought, therefore, that the issue is relative only to the possibility of language. It has, however, wider implications than that; it is an issue about the conditions for a common understanding, something that is implicit in language as a means of communication. That common understanding is a presupposition of knowledge, and if anyone, human or animal, is to know he must enter into it. When Wittgenstein says that this in turn presupposes agreement in judgments, he adds that this seems to overthrow logic, but that it does not really do so. It seems to do so because it makes the intelligibility of language in terms of which truths are to be formulated depend on the prior acceptance of things as so; so the intelligibility on which the truth depends seems to presuppose truth.[14] If there is a paradox in this its solution lies in the recognition that agreement in judgments means, as Wittgenstein puts it, agreement in forms of life. Elsewhere (*Philosophical Investigations*, p. 226) he says that it is forms of life that constitute the given, as it were. I take him to mean that they constitute the given and necessarily accepted framework against which alone questions about what is so and not so can be raised. They thus constitute in some sense the limits within which we can speak of what is and what is not. If this is so, there are Kantian echoes in the thesis, although whether Wittgenstein explicitly intended such echoes need not be our present concern. The important point is that the notion of agreement in judgments must be interpreted in such a way that the agreement is seen to be relative to and against the background of an agreement of a wider and somehow more practical kind. The question whether animals can agree with us in judgment is thus of a part with the question whether they can share our form of life. Only through this last question, therefore, can we make any approach to the question of whether we can attach sense to the idea that animals might know what it is for something to be true or false. To say that an animal can share our form of life is to say at least that its behaviour is intelligible to us and that it fits in with what we do in a way that is at least consistent with the way in which what other *people* do may fit in with what we do. This presupposes at the very least a sensibility in common with us, common forms of judgment, and equally common forms of expression; i.e., at least the possibility of taking the world in similar or analogous ways to that in which *we* take it on the basis of the operation of the senses.

I do not think, however, that this is sufficient. What I have said so far need imply no more than a *coincidence* in ways of behaving; it need entail no more than analogies between animal and human behaviour, and the question of whether an animal has anything like a human consciousness could never be clinched by such analogies. Nor do I think that the agreement implied in what I have said would be a true agreement. For our purpose there must be a real community of life, and for this to be possible we have to bring into consideration wants, interests, feelings and the like. That is indeed obvious as soon as one comes to think of it. The intelligibility of the behaviour of other human beings as well as that of animals presupposes that there are between them common, although of course sometimes conflicting, wants and interests. The community has to be real in the sense that the common interests must potentially be the same and not just similar in kind. Many organisms take in food, even seek it in some sense of the word 'seek', equally as they seek the means of reproduction; but it is worth noting that we do not normally think that enough to justify the attribution of consciousness to them, nor enough to speak of their having knowledge of any kind. Even in the case of animals where there are considerable analogies between their and our behaviour (e.g., ants) we may with justification have doubts about their possession of consciousness. This is so, I suggest, because their interests, etc. do not really impinge on ours, even when they are similar in kind or appear to be similar in kind to ours, e.g., in the requirement of food. For an animal's interests really to impinge on ours, it must be capable of seeing other creatures or humans *as* creatures with interests of this kind. It must therefore be capable of standing in relation to such other creatures in ways that have something in common with the ways in which we may stand in relation to each other.

It is in fact this last point which, I suggest, provides for the possibility of correction in domestic animals, and to the extent that this is practicable in wild animals also. I said earlier that the possibility of an animal or a child learning from correction depends on the animal or child taking the correction *as* correction. It now becomes clear that this is possible only if in turn the animal or child sees the corrector as a person or, where the corrector is an animal, something close to a person. For this to be possible, the animal or child has to stand in relations to something like a personal kind to the teacher or corrector. It would not be much of an exaggeration to say that one all-important factor in the development of children as persons is that they are treated as persons by persons. We can speak of an animal knowing things, and therefore recognising things as being so or not so, only to the extent that we can contemplate the possibility of its standing in a relation of this kind to us. I say 'only to the extent' and I would emphasise the 'only'. I am concerned here only with the necessary conditions for speaking of knowledge in connection with animals; I say nothing here about the sufficient conditions. It is possible, however, to generalise about the necessary conditions. It would seem that a necessary condition of anything's being said to have knowledge (and perception too, since perception presupposes knowledge in at least the form of concepts) is that it is possible for it to stand in relations to us in the way that I have indicated. We cannot fully understand the possibility of such knowledge unless we see those who have knowledge in the framework of such relations (relations which, as I have argued, cannot be merely cognitive). What emerges from all this is the connection between such concepts as those of knowledge, truth, learning, the possibility of correction, common interests or wants, and thus the possibility of standing in relation to other beings in ways which are at least akin to human relations. It would seem, therefore, that we shall not fully understand such 'epistemological' notions as those of knowledge and understanding unless and until we see them in the framework of and against the background of the relationships in which we stand to each other and to other things.[15]

I noted earlier in this book that traditional epistemology, since at least Descartes, has tended to present the problems as if they were such that the individual has to solve them by himself without reference to others; it has presented men as solitary centres of consciousness for whom the fundamental problem is the construction of a world including other men, and this is a problem that each man has to solve on his own. It should be clear that the terms of reference in which such problems are presented are such that they really presuppose for their intelligibility the prior existence of a community in which the members recognise each other at any rate to the extent that they see each other as sharing common interests and concerns. This itself comes about, I suggest, through an upbringing in which the relations in which a young child or animal stands to adults, and parents in particular, are of paramount importance. The part that genetic and other causal factors play in this varies from creature to creature, and it is very evident that they loom larger in the case of animals than in the case of humans, even if for humans too they are indispensable. Nevertheless, the part played in upbringing by relations with others is vital, where there is to be any case for speaking of the creature in question as acquiring and developing knowledge.

I have discussed animals in such detail because their case brings out in a particularly acute form what must be presupposed if concepts are to be attributed to anything. Much of what I have said of animals can be transferred to the case of human children, as I have indicated already in effect. Just as we can ask the question under what general conditions an animal can be said to have the conceptual understanding and knowledge which is both a precondition of experience and in some way its product, so we can ask about the general conditions which makes development of the same thing possible in the human child. In this respect the pre-linguistic human child is in the same position as the animal. While the human child is potentially far more intelligent than the animal and less dependent on those factors which one may call 'instinct', the development of that intelligence in the ways that will make possible the eventual emergence of the language-using capacity depends on, among other things, the satisfaction of the same conditions that make animal intelligence and the capacity for its use possible in their own way. The comparative slowness of the infant's development is a function of its greater intelligence, its lesser dependence on instinctual factors, and its greater dependence on relations with adults than holds good with the young animal. (Even in the case of animals, however, much may depend on the presence of the mother at certain crucial times in the young animal's development, as is shown by the phenomenon of 'imprinting' studied by ethologists.)

Thus an understanding of how experience is possible, whether in humans or in animals, must involve also an understanding not only of the causal conditions for it, both genetic and environmental, but also of how knowledge and conceptual understanding become possible and get application under these conditions. In discussing perception in the previous chapter I tried to say something about the relations between knowledge and causal conditions in perception itself (although I have no doubt that there is much more to be said). In this chapter I have tried to indicate that the possibility of knowledge itself, including the knowledge that is involved in having concepts, is something that presupposes not only again the satisfaction of causal conditions, partly genetic partly environmental, but also the sharing in a common form of life. The implications of this last notion suggest that a creature that can know must also be a creature capable of other things. It must have wants and interests in common with others in such a way that these are really common, if often competing. This in turn implies the possibility of seeing others as such, and this cannot take place unless the creature in question is in a position to have relations with others, relations that may be founded on feeling or are at any rate not simply cognitive in nature.

In sum, without the possibility of knowledge there would be no experience (for while knowledge need not precede experience in time, it is a logically necessary condition of experience and the latter cannot precede it entirely). There could, however, be no possibility of knowledge without the possibility of agreement over what is so and what is not so. This presupposes common reactions and attitudes to the world, something which, in the sense of 'reaction' and 'attitude' in question, presupposes in turn common, though sometimes competing, interests and wants. Hence, knowledge and experience would be impossible except in creatures which have such interests; except, that is, in creatures which have feelings, and feelings which involve each other as well as other things. In the next chapter I shall apply these considerations to the problem of how knowledge and understanding come about in the individual child.

7   The beginnings of understanding

A natural reaction perhaps to what I have said so far would be: 'That is all very well, but how does it actually happen?' The protest would be a reflection of the fact that in trying to say something about the necessary conditions for the growth of experience, knowledge and understanding, I have been working at a level of extreme generality; it might be argued that it is now time that the account was pinned down to cases. I would respect the protest, although it is important to be clear about what it would entail. There is a sense in which the question might be taken in which it is one properly to be aimed at a psychologist, not a philosopher. On that interpretation it would be a demand for some of the facts about infant development, and perhaps for some account of the ways in which that development is to be seen as taking place. If it is taken in that way, it may be that the only quick answer to the question of how it all takes place is 'in many different ways'; and then the psychologist and the expert in child development may take over. I have no particular expertise in such an area and I shall not, therefore, make any attempt to answer the question if taken in that sense. To respond in that way is not, however, to shuffle off responsibility, since there is another way of taking the question which I shall try to deal with. This way of taking the question is to interpret it as a request that the various conditions that I have mentioned should be related to each other with reference to possible cases, so that a story emerges about it all which is at least coherent. It is still not clear, for example, how what I have said about the importance of recognising the part played by feelings and attitudes links on to the more traditionally epistemological aspects of the story. All that I have said on that theme is that knowledge cannot exist without something like the concept of truth; and that cannot exist except in creatures which are capable of interrelationships that have something of the character of the personal. It might also be maintained that I have equally said that those interrelationships presuppose some idea of what a person is. How does that come about, and what is its exact relation to the other concepts that a child comes to have?

Let me emphasise again, in connection with this last point, that a philosopher can have nothing to say, *qua* philosopher, about the temporal ordering of forms of understanding. He can be concerned only with the logical presuppositions of any given form of understanding, what must be the case *if* it is to exist; and the only conclusions about temporal ordering that could be drawn from that would be about what *cannot* be the case. The point that I want to make concerning the dependence of knowledge on something like the concept of a person (to put the matter very roughly) is on a par with, although not identical with, Kant's claim in the Transcendental Deduction of his *Critique of Pure Reason* that awareness of objects with an identity in space and time is correlative with awareness of oneself as a self. Kant's thesis has no necessary implications for the temporal ordering of those forms of awareness and understanding; nor has mine. Hence, when it is asked what is the exact relation of the concept of a person to the other concepts that a child comes to have, it is not temporal relations that should be our present concern. What is required is further details concerning what it is that makes this particular concept a logical presupposition of the others.

Before I go into this issue, I want to say something to meet another possible objection: that I have done nothing to stop the regress implied, as I said at the beginning of this book, by the idea that the acquisition of knowledge implies already existing knowledge. Since having a concept implies knowledge and presupposes knowledge, it might seem that *no* concept can be acquired without pre-existing knowledge. Where does that ultimately come from, if innate knowledge is ruled out? And ruled out it must be by the considerations that I raised in the last chapter, as I suggested it would be at the end of chapter 3. To attribute innate knowledge to something, we should have to suppose that it had that knowledge immediately when born, if not before, when *ex hypothesi* the conditions which would make it a possible stander in relations to us were missing. It is important to be clear about what is being said in this. Such a consideration does not preclude altogether our saying of something in certain circumstances that it knows instinctively such and such. There is no objection to such a way of speaking; it is merely to say that the creature in question knows whatever it is without having learnt it. Provided that the creature satisfied the condition of being a possible sharer in our form of life, we might have grounds for ascribing knowledge to it, even if we had no evidence of its having learnt it. That would not be possible if it never learnt *anything*, since it could not then be a possible sharer in *our* form of life. A hypothetical possessor of innate knowledge must, however, be in that very position at some point, that is to say at least when just born. Innate knowledge would imply having the concept of truth or something like it without the possibility of being a party to that agreement without which the concept of truth could get no purchase.

Whatever be the correct analysis of the concept of knowledge, the knower must be capable of getting things right, and this must not be just a happy accident. Moreover, getting things right means getting them right by public, inter-subjective and objective standards. If the 'innate knower' achieved this it could only be a happy accident, and this would preclude its being real knowledge that he possessed. Even in the cases of 'instinctive knowledge' that I have referred to we presuppose that there is *some* explanation of how the person or animal knows, even if we exclude learning. Such cases are nevertheless derivative cases and would be unintelligible if they were the norm; that is to say that we should refuse to attribute *knowledge* if the person or animal were like that in general. Thus in animals where instinct is everything, we do not explain the fittingness of the behaviour by referring to what the animal knows; rather, we explain the behaviour in more mechanical terms, or at least in biological terms, by reference to its role in the preservation of the species, as is typical in biology in general and ethology in particular.

I have not in this said that the knower must actually be a party to inter-subjective agreement, only that he, she or it must be a possible party to this. Otherwise animal knowledge would be made impossible. The very community in forms of life, however, between animals and ourselves makes them, as I tried to show in the last chapter, subject to possible correction, and this correction can, for the same reason, be correction as we understand it; and this, as I have also tried to show, presupposes a sensitivity to the possibility of being right and wrong. Hence all these ideas go together, and their application presents no difficulty where learning has gone on or is at least possible. The difficulties are, however, insuperable where learning is not in court at all. At the same time, it should be noted that the consequent impossibility of innate knowledge by no means rules out other innate factors in humans and animals: an inborn constitution and thus inborn powers, tendencies and dispositions. Without these a common form of life would itself be impossible. It is innate *knowledge* that the considerations that I have adduced rule out.

If, however, it *is* ruled out, how does the growth of knowledge start? There are a number of important issues here, some of which I have mentioned already. To fit them into a coherent and illuminating story is difficult, immensely difficult. If I do not succeed in presenting such a story in a way that is completely adequate, it is to be hoped nevertheless that the account will be indicative of what is at stake. One of the problems is the near, if not absolute, impossibility of sloughing off adult modes of thought in trying to get into the child's mind; another is what is indeed perhaps the absolute impossibility of giving anything like a complete account of child thought in adult terms, even if this must be attempted in some part in writing for adults.

It is perhaps best to start with the important observation that not all acquisition of knowledge need be learning. Even in the case of adults we sometimes speak of their having come to know something without necessarily implying that they have learnt it, even if these cases are again exceptions to the general rule. There are inspired guesses, inspirations, insights and the like. I do not mention these to suggest that the dawning of a child's consciousness can be appropriately described in these terms, since the terms are ones that we use against the background of our ordinary and more pedestrian understanding of human knowledge. Nevertheless, it is possible for us to come to take things in a certain way without this being counted by us or recognised by us as knowledge, and yet for it to be recognised later that this is what it indeed was. We may say 'I came to know at that point that it was so, although I did not recognise at the time that I did know it'. I want to emphasise this point, since it follows from it that there is certainly no need for us to assume that if the child comes to know something he must know or be aware that he does know whatever it is. Provided—and this is an extremely important proviso—the child is in a position to have knowledge at all, then if he or she distinguishes between X and Y (in whatever way this is revealed in behaviour), if there is indeed a difference between X and Y, and if the child's distinguishing X and Y is not a chance event (however this too is revealed in the behaviour of the child in the circumstances), then we might well have sufficient grounds for saying that he or she has come to know the difference between X and Y.

I rely in what I have said on traditional, if often disputed, analyses of knowledge which connect knowledge with true belief which is justified or at least not a chance matter. Whether or not that analysis is sufficient does not matter very much for present purposes; it is sufficient that if the conditions mentioned are satisfied we might in certain circumstances be justified in speaking of knowledge. On the other hand, to say that the child has learnt that X and Y are different would be to imply rather more: that the child has come through experience to connect this point with other things that he or she knows, and that these other things are the basis of the learning. One might indeed say that learning is connecting items of knowledge in the way specified, whereas not all this is implied in simply coming to know. It is a plausible thesis that no item of knowledge can exist by itself, that atomism in knowledge is false (for the same reason that there cannot be atomic propositions: that any given proposition always has implications and stands in a web of such implications because the meanings of the terms in which it is expressed equally do not stand by themselves)[1]. This would suggest that any acquisition of knowledge involves the connecting of items of which I have spoken. In learning, however, the connection is between what one comes to know and what one knows *already*, so that it is right to say what I said earlier: that learning implies knowledge which is pre-existent in time. There are no such necessary implications with coming to know *simpliciter*, even if coming to know involves connecting things; that is to say that in the case of simple coming to know there are no *temporal* implications about the connecting.

At least two possible objections might be made to this. First, it might be objected that I made above an important proviso: the child must be in the position to have knowledge. Without this the satisfaction of the other conditions mentioned will not provide sufficient grounds for speaking of knowledge. What I mean is that the child must be a potential knower in the sense that he or she, like the animals of the last chapter, must be in the position to accept truth as truth, and this must be in the position to be mistaken and to recognise correction as correction. In the last chapter I mentioned the essential condition that candidates for knowledge in this sense must stand or be capable of standing in relations to us. I shall have more to say about that later in this chapter. If I do not go into more detail about it at this stage it is because my primary concern now is with the ordering of knowledge, *given that knowledge is possible*. It must be remembered throughout, however, that the story presented presupposes that the child is a *child* who has been and is being brought up in a context of very personal relations; he is not a simple classifier or discriminater. It is not possible to attribute knowledge to the child, not even knowledge about other persons, unless he or she is capable of responding to persons in a personal way. Once again, however, we should not think of the process as one in which the child first enters into personal relations and then makes discriminations which may in that case, if other conditions are satisfied, amount to knowledge. The different aspects of the process take their course together. The important *logical* point is that discriminations will not count as knowledge, even when the other conditions mentioned are satisfied, unless the child is more than a discriminater, unless he is a human child capable of response to and of getting responses from adult human beings, such responses being themselves of a specific human kind. I shall return to this issue later in the chapter, but I shall concentrate for the time being on the discriminations themselves and the ways in which these involve knowledge, if the general conditions are satisfied.

Second, it might be objected to what I have said about the child coming to distinguish X and Y, that he could not distinguish X and Y without knowing something of what X and Y are, and thus that he must have to some extent or other the concepts of X and Y. In that case, if having the concepts of X and Y is to be construed in terms of knowing what it is for something to be X and Y (and I think that it must), the child must have other knowledge than that referred to in saying that he has come to distinguish X and Y; he must know what it is for something to be X and know what it is for something to be Y. In one way this thesis is consistent with what I have said about the non-atomic character of knowledge; the child cannot know the difference between X and Y without knowing other things, and there is no need to think that the 'without' implies the temporal precedence of that other knowledge. Yet it might be argued that there is still a problem here, since one might be inclined to believe that knowing what X and Y are is likely to emerge from and be based upon a knowledge of the difference between X and Y rather than vice versa. To put the matter in other ways, there cannot be a difference which does not imply some respect in which the difference exists, and seeing the difference seems to imply seeing it in the respect in which it exists; but to know the respect in which X and Y differ is to know already something about what X and Y are, so that the distinguishing of X and Y cannot be the foundation of that knowledge. How can one come to know what X and Y are through experience, when the very distinguishing of them in experience implies knowing what they are; that is to say, it implies already the concepts of X and Y?

The solution to the problem lies in seeing once again that the knowledge involved in having a concept of something admits of degrees. For the child to distinguish X and Y, there has to be a respect in which the difference is seen, but the child need not know that respect. To know the respect he would have, among other things, to see the difference between it and other respects. Hence, while there has to be a respect in which X and Y differ, if they are to be seen as different, the child does not have to know that respect. Yet in seeing the difference between X and Y the child does know something about what it is for something to be X and for something to be Y; he knows that they are *different* without necessarily knowing anything more about them. It might be objected that this does not amount to much of a concept of X or a concept of Y. That is true, but it would be false to say that it is no concept at all. To gain further knowledge the child has to see other differences at varying levels. Yet even at the level at which the child simply sees a difference between X and Y he does thereby also know something of what X and Y are; and he might come to know this without that knowledge being founded on other knowledge of a previously existing kind, in the way in which it would have to be if coming to know were always the same as learning.[2]

The issues here have to do with the relations between understanding and experience, a subject on which I have had things to say in the last two chapters. Experience, in the perceptual sense, is nothing without some understanding, even if it has sensation as its condition. It is not necessary, however, to suppose that the understanding is prior to the experience in time. What is requisite is an account of an elementary experience which is compatible with the claim that in having it the child has understanding, without any prior understanding being presupposed. This I have tried to give. In the experience the child comes to know something, and this cannot be construed as learning since learning does presuppose that the child builds on what is already known. That, however, does not prevent its being a case of coming to know. Moreover, it is important to resist here the idea that one is 'given' in the experience a unit of knowledge that along with other such units can be built up into complex structures. It is this that I have rejected in rejecting the idea that knowledge can have an atomic character as its basis. Hence it remains true that one cannot know or come to know one thing without knowing something else; but that 'without' need not imply a priority in time for that 'something else'. That would be necessary for learning but not for coming to know *simpliciter*. If what the whole structure of experience and understanding develops from can be something at the level of a simple discrimination, there is still understanding of a kind in the experience that that discrimination involves. This is because X and Y cannot be distinguished without something thereby being known of X and Y; and conversely one cannot know anything of X except in contrast to something—in this case Y.

Thus in seeing and knowing the difference between X and Y the child knows something of what X and Y are, and this provides the basis for the acquisition through learning of other knowledge of X and Y, and thereby also of other things. This will reflect back upon the difference between X and Y, so that in the course of learning the child comes to know more of the difference between X and Y. This sort of point becomes very important later in the child's life, when one is called upon, as one is in connection with Piaget's conservation studies, to answer the question whether a child can understand what it is for something to have a physical identity and yet not understand all the circumstances in which something of this kind can and cannot change its volume: a liquid changes in volume when heated, but not when poured into a broader vessel so that its level changes.Clearly a child can know something about identity without knowing these other things; yet when it does know these other things it will know more about identity, so that the knowledge which it acquires reflects back upon the knowledge that it started with. There are indeed degrees of knowledge, no matter what the object of knowledge is. It is perhaps worth noting in this context that Piaget sometimes describes his method as the 'relational method' and his general thesis as a form of structuralism. The implication is that the growth of understanding is a matter of more and more complex structures and relationships. Such a notion must not be used, however, in such a way as to imply that the elements of the structures are ultimately 'given'. In distinguishing X and Y I certainly relate X and Y and thereby arrive at a construal of X and Y, but that construal need not be taken as a constant; subsequent learning may lead, as I have said, to a reflection back upon it which may alter its whole character. Piaget's notion of 'horizontal displacement of structures'—the fact that at a given stage knowledge of one aspect of things may be displaced from knowledge of other aspects—gives too hard and fast an impression of the structures themselves. It may prevent a recognition of the important point that I have laboured: that knowledge and understanding admit of degrees.

I have not in all this, however, tried to say anything about what sort of thing X and Y might be in the earliest part of a child's life, or about how the child comes to fasten on things of this kind. The fatal and wrong suggestion is that the child starts by distinguishing its own experience, because if the child is initially confined to its experiences there is no way out of this so that it can come to have knowledge of a world independent of itself. It could not even come to have any conception of such a world. On the other hand, anything that it could be aware of must initially be undifferentiated. William James described it as a blooming, buzzing confusion, but that description really applies to the experience as it would be to an adult presented with a similar situation without knowledge of what it is all about; it is the kind of description that might be offered by an adult with reference to an utterly new, but multi-coloured and changing state of affairs. It is an indication of bewilderment. The child, however, is in its earliest life not sophisticated enough even to be bewildered; with no preconceptions there is nothing to be bewildered about. James's description illustrates the difficulty of getting into the child's mind with adult ideas of it and adult forms of description.

I have said that anything that the young child can be aware of must be initially undifferentiated; that is to say that it will be for the child nothing in particular and everything in general. It is doubtful, however, if that can really be true, since the human child is born with a natural constitution which brings with it natural dispositions and ways of response to things. Given this and the fact that the world into which it is born provides such vast possibilities of differentiation the child must inevitably have its attention fastened on some things rather than others. Hence some differences will be immediately forced upon it. Much in what follows this depends upon what it is put in the way of in this manner, and it is very important that adult treatment constitutes a kind of channelling of attention, without which the child would in all probability not develop in any way, whether psychological or physical. Some of this may be true of some animals too, although in their case much more depends upon the inborn tendencies and dispositions to react to features of the world. The human child is by no means infinitely plastic, even if experience matters much more than is the case with many animals.

If then one returns to the question of what kinds of thing the X and Y might be in the earliest part of a child's life, there is no clear answer. If one attempts to answer within the terms of reference provided by such categories as experience or physical object, one will be using concepts that get no purchase on a baby's consciousness. If, as has often been claimed, there is for the new-born baby no distinction between self and non-self, the difficulties are magnified even further. It is not easy to assess that claim, but it is at any rate clear that, to follow Kant, awareness when achieved of objects with an independent existence in space and time as anything like what they actually are is correlative with awareness of oneself as both subject and agent. It is noteworthy that, as many psychologists have maintained, the earliest part of a child's life is that part in which physical, motor and manipulative skills develop. The part played in this connection by inborn constitution and maturation must be immense, but given these factors learning brings with it some conception of objects as manipulative or resistent to such manipulation, and of oneself as a manipulator successful or unsuccessful. That is to say that experience provides in this way conditions which make those kinds of awareness *possible*. How they actually produce those kinds of awareness and whether it is right to suggest that they do are further questions. What is clear is that these things, together with what the child is put in the way of by adults, put him also in the way of making further distinctions within the objects of consciousness, distinctions that would not be possible without them.

It is far from clear, however, whether any of this is sufficient if the distinction between self and non-self is to emerge. To suppose that it is sufficient may be to approach too close to the conception of the child as a little experimenter or explorer seeking to find out how much of what lies within his consciousness is really him, by finding out how much he can manipulate and how much he cannot. It is a fact of some importance that the child's upbringing is an initiation into a world as circumscribed by other human beings. It is part of the acquisition of what we call the objective view of the world that the child should enter into the human form of life. Relations with other human beings must therefore be of paramount importance. These, however, will not be possible unless he possesses already the potentiality for being human; that is to say unless he is a human child with a physical constitution that is capable of developing into an adult human one. What is important about this is that the child must be capable of responding to human attention of varying kinds in ways that are also human. Let us try to get clear about what that means.

Two extremes to be avoided here in the attempt to form a proper conception of the infant's relation to other human beings are what might be called the purely mechanical model and the model of the child as a source of practical reason. As far as the first is concerned, I am indeed inclined to believe (although considering our present state of knowledge this is little more than an act of faith, so to speak) that it must be possible in principle to give an account of the course of an organism's interaction with its environment in purely physiological and physical terms. Whether or not that is true, it does not of itself imply that the *child's* relationship to the world (including other persons) is to be construed in a similarly mechanical way. To say that some part of

97

the child's body reacts in some way or reveals a pattern of reaction over time in response to some form of stimulation does not entail that it is correct to speak of the *child* reacting similarly. Or rather, if one does wish to use the term 'react' in this context, it will have shifted its sense, in such a way that the 'reaction' is not necessarily to be construed in purely mechanical terms. The ramifications of this issue are vast, and presuppose all the considerations that arise from the mind-body problem and the way in which the concept of a person enters into this. The issues have been much discussed by philosophers in recent times. This is not the place at which to enter into a detailed discussion of those issues; it is sufficient to note that the possibility of 'mechanism' at the level of physiology and physics (assuming that it is indeed a possibility) does not necessarily imply that the child's relationships with other people and the world in general are to be construed in those terms. The *child's* relation to, say, its mother is not to be construed simply on the model of stimulus and response, even if its *body* is receiving and reacting to stimuli throughout.

On the other hand, it is equally important not to read into the child's relations with others or with things straightforwardly adult attitudes. As far as things are concerned, the child's attitude to them in the earliest part of his life must be simply manipulative, but not in the sense that he treats them merely as objects for use, as would be suggested if we spoke similarly of adult attitudes. It is rather that things initially figure largely, if not exclusively, as objects of touch and feeling, and as something that calls out bodily movements of one kind or another; so much so, that physical objects must eventually acquire an identity and character for the child in a context of this kind. It is still less plausible to view the child's initial and early relationship with other human beings as manipulative in the adult sense, although once again feeling, touch and bodily movement must figure large in that relationship. It is equally implausible to construe the child's attitudes to others as a product of anything calculating or a concern for practical reason. It is not, for example, that the child recognises that the treatment that it receives is of a certain kind, such that it merits a similar reply.[3] If the child responds to love with eventual love on its own part it cannot be that this is the result of a recognition that this response is the appropriate one in the circumstances. That would demand an understanding of what is involved in a relationship which is both too complex and something that one would expect perhaps to emerge out of its first responses rather than to be a presupposition of them.

What I have said about these two extremes applies also to

hedonism as a theory of what governs the way in which learned behaviour comes about. Hedonism has been put forward as a theory of the springs of human behaviour, either as part of a story in which the model is a mechanical one involving only pushes and pulls, or as more or less the whole story about practical rationality. In its first form, the idea is that pleasure acts merely as a reinforcing tendency with pain as its opposite; it plays, that is, a role in the context of other mechanistic processes of promoting certain of these processes rather than others. At the level at which it is perhaps appropriate to speak of mechanism—the physiological level—such a theory is too crude, to say the least. It would have to be interpreted as saying that when certain kinds of processes are touched off there is a tendency for other kinds of processes to be perpetuated. It seems doubtful whether the mechanisms could be as simple as that, but in any case such an interpretation removes the one feature that makes hedonism attractive. Hedonism is nothing unless it presents a thesis about human or animal motivation, and a purely mechanical story says nothing about that. On that theory the rationale of the perpetuation of the tendencies in question would be purely mechanical and nothing would necessarily be implied about the *significance* of the feelings for the person or animal concerned; that is to say that nothing in the mechanical story would necessarily suggest that the processes were perpetuated because they or something connected with them *were pleasant*.

At the other extreme, hedonism is the thesis that pleasure is the supreme end for human beings, so that what they do in general is done with a view to its contribution to the production of pleasure. To suppose that the child is governed by the principles of hedonism in this sense is to suppose that it is concerned with things and what it does as means to pleasure. The objections that apply here are the same as those which I adduced earlier against the suggestion that one could construe the child's developing attitudes as governed by considerations of practical reason. The thesis in question would imply too sophisticated a set of concepts on the part of the child, and as a basis for the development of an understanding of its relationship with others and with other things it would presuppose just that which it is trying to explain. The calculation of means to pleasure would presuppose an understanding of the relationships in terms of which things can be seen as means, and could not therefore be used to explain how that understanding comes about. Pleasure is no doubt a motivating factor in the development of the child's attitudes, but it cannot be this in either of the ways reviewed.

The relationship that the child has with others need not, however, be construed in terms of either of the extremes that I have noted; its attitudes need not be either caused and brought about in a mechanical way or adopted by the child as part of the exercise of practical reason. To suppose that they must be one or other of these things is to suppose that human beings must be construed either as completely rational in a full-blooded sense or as mere products of stimulation and reaction to this. I said earlier that the child must be capable of responding to human attention in ways that are also human; I have since then tried to indicate what that does *not* mean. Some of the child's reactions will no doubt be mechanical, as it were; none of them will be the result of practical reason; but many will be neither. Human beings have attitudes to things which are, in a broad sense of the word, 'emotional'. A certain pattern of expression of feeling in one individual may call out other or similar expressions of feeling in another, or at any rate may produce a disposition to such expression. This is part of our natural and inherited constitution, modifiable though it is by learning through experience or by rational control or inhibition. The ethologists have pointed out that in many animals quite complex patterns of behaviour may be triggered off by relatively and sometimes extremely restricted environmental conditions (for the explanation of which we should have to look, of course, to evolutionary theory and the part played by the pattern of behaviour in relation to the species). We have no reason to doubt the existence of such tendencies in human beings, even if they loom less large and are much more plastic than in the case of animals. However that may be, one ought not to fight shy of thinking of human beings as possessing natural forms of expression of an emotional kind, the emergence and perpetuation of which may in some cases be dependent on those human beings' being treated in appropriate ways. Thus the expression of love by parents may naturally elicit expressions of love in return, not because the child sees this as an appropriate thing to do, but because it just has this propensity naturally.[4]

In a context of this kind the child will have his attention directed in ways that would not be so if he were simply dependent on the contingencies of experience, as empiricists have supposed must be the case. At the same time it is not right to think of what happens simply as the product of an interaction between the individual's innate structure and the structuring influences to which he is subject because of the expression of his innate tendencies. So far we should not have got beyond a Piagetian interactionism, and would not have met the objections to this that I noted in chapter 4 and have rehearsed again to some extent in this chapter. The other people who treat the child in ways that are relevant to his development are not just one aspect of the world among others. It is not just that the child is enabled, because of the channelling of his attention, to distinguish from each other a variety of things including people. It is important that the influences that other people bring to bear must be seen as in an important sense educational. They must bring it about, not just that the child makes distinctions, but that he makes the distinctions *that really hold good*; this is part of the process through which there emerges the concept of truth, which is vital if the child is to have knowledge as such. If this is to be achieved the child must be subject to correction and he must take this as correction, something that would not be possible did he not in some way recognise the correctors as just that. This in turn entails seeing them as people with intentions and wants of their own, yet people who share a common form of life. How is all this made possible by the story that I have told so far?

It is impossible to answer that question if it is taken as a demand for a chart of the course by which the child's understanding arrives at this point; it is clear that it takes the growing child a considerable time and that there may be many variations in the course taken. Piaget has argued that, in the so-called moral development of the child, the second stage (that of going by strict moral rules) arises out of a previous stage when for the child 'right' is what parents or grown-ups generally say or demand. All this occurs at a much later stage of the child's general development than the period that I am considering now; but we may perhaps suppose, to use Piagetian language, a 'filiation' between that later course of development and that which takes place in the earliest period of the child's life. The filiation will exist for a good reason: that the appreciation of rules (something that is integral to an appreciation of what is correct and incorrect, so and not so, true and false, as well as right and wrong) is likely to emerge out of an appreciation of 'what *they* want'. I mean that the child has to come to accept the existence of other interests, wants, wishes, feelings and attitudes, sometimes agreeing, but often not, with his own. Indeed this would be an important part of coming to recognise the existence of other persons. Hence again the importance of personal relationships based on such feelings and attitudes. The recognition of other persons is very much a matter of the recognition of them as sources of feelings and attitudes of various kinds, which fit in with or conflict with the child's own in a great variety of ways. It is no exaggeration to say that the treatment of the child progressively as a person, and therefore as both the recipient and source of human feelings and attitudes, is of vital importance in the child's becoming a person in a real sense. Indeed, it might be said that there is a stage at which the world is for the child just a mass of feeling; for development as a person those feelings will have to be directed to the child in certain ways and his own feelings will thus be educated also. (If the world is initially this source of feeling, the 'animism' that many have seen in the thought of the young child is not surprising.)

The child's structuring of his environment, granted his own innate tendencies and capacities, must therefore be seen in a context of this kind. It is not just that he comes to see similarities and differences (although he no doubt does just this), but that some of these are given importance by the roles which they play in relationships with others, particularly of course his mother or whoever it is that is responsible for the child's nurture in a given culture. Thus what is so and not so come to be, as we in adult ways of speaking would say, 'what *they* want and do not want'. That is of course far too crude as it stands, since it cannot be nearly as simple as that; and we are incapable of any exact appreciation of the likely subtleties of the growth of a child's consciousness. What *is* important is that we should not, in trying to gain an understanding of what a growing consciousness must be like, view the child as a purely cognitive entity, as something merely engaged in discrimination and classification, like a computer when programmed and fed with information in the right way. Although it is important that the child has innate tendencies and capacities (the programming) and that its attention is channelled so that it is put in the way of things (the data fed into it), it could never thereby, any more than a computer could, come to an understanding of what it is for things to be so and not so, of what it is to be correct and incorrect. That could come only through relations with others in which feelings, wants and attitudes play a large part. Hence emotion is not simply a distracting and irrational factor; it is an essential component in intellectual development. An essential stage in the acquisition of knowledge of what it is for something to be X is, through this: distinguishing Xs 'as *they* do'.

Language 8

The kind of point that I made in the last chapter must also have applications to the learning of language. Children do not normally learn to talk until about the age of two, and much has gone on in the interval that must be relevant to the acquisition of that specific capacity. I make that point because some, including Chomsky, have seemed to argue as if one could consider language learning by itself without reference to the background from which it must emerge. Thus Chomsky has claimed that what is essential to linguistic competence—the capacity for coping with what is common to all languages and which therefore involves linguistic universals—cannot be derived from the data available to the child, since the data are 'corrupt' and therefore insufficient for the purpose; it is claimed in consequence that the capacity must be innate. This view involves many assumptions, as well as a model of the learning process which I have repudiated in the foregoing; the child cannot be conceived as set over against the world, trying to make sense of it. For present purposes, however, the point on which I wish to concentrate is that one cannot consider the child's acquisition of language as if it can be divorced from the other things that the child has learnt and is still learning, and also from the other features of its life.

I have had something to say about Chomsky's theory earlier in chapter 3. I indicated there that included among the categories of deep structure (knowledge of which Chomsky supposes to be fundamental to linguistic competence, and on the basis of which the surface structure of any particular language is learned) are those of subject and predicate. In effect Chomsky is claiming in this that human beings know innately what it is to say something about something else, or at any rate what it is for something to be said of something else. In reply to Chomsky's general claim for the innateness of knowledge of linguistic universals, Piaget has argued that language emerges out of 'symbolic functions';[1] language, that is, is one use of symbols, and the understanding of language is a specific form of the understanding of symbols. On this view the understanding of language is prefigured in an earlier symbolic understanding. The notion of 'prefiguration' as used in this context is suggestive, but more would be required of it, if Chomsky's argument is to be met, than a mere reference to symbolic function. What, for example, would correspond in this to the distinction between subject and predicate? The notions of grammar and of grammatical structure are crucial for Chomsky's view of language, and he argues persuasively in the last chapter of *Language and Mind* against the idea that the possession of language is equivalent merely to the capacity for the use of understanding of symbols. If the notion of prefiguration is to do any work, therefore, grammatical distinctions also must be prefigured in the pre-linguistic child's experience.

If it is possible to find such prefiguration it is not that the child has to abstract ideas such as those of subject and predicate from the data available to him. We need not accept that way of looking at the problem in order to reply to Chomsky; and if we are unable to make provision for such abstraction we are not thereby thrown into the camp of innate ideas. In seeking to show, in the account that I have given already, how the child learns from experience, I have not wanted to suggest either of these points of view, and I have in any case made criticisms of them in earlier chapters. Rather, the correct suggestion must be that relevant experience enables the child to form something like the ideas of subject and predicate, etc., so that the knowledge in question may, so to speak, be given flesh in learning. By the age at which language emerges children are, in any case, given to much active experimentation in relation to the world as they find it, and it is well known that many children jabber away, before learning to speak in the proper way, in sounds that have something linguistic about them. In such cases, we might justifiably say that the child has got something of the idea of what language is: the use of sounds as a means of communication. Nevertheless, communication as such has, of course, gone on in other ways for long before this.

I would like to emphasise this last point. Parents communicate with pre-linguistic children by gestures, actions and expressions, as well as by talking to them; they show them things, direct their movements and correct what they do. Above all perhaps, in the earliest days, they express and thereby communicate feelings by their responses to the child. It is in the context of this sort of thing that we must see the understanding of language eventually emerging. The grammatical notions of subject and predicate correspond in their use to those of drawing attention to something (perhaps by an indicative device or an expression the conventional use of which has this function at least) and of expressing something about it. In a communicative act, however, drawing attention to something could scarcely exist by itself without its being implied that something was being expressed about the thing in question. I say 'expressed' rather than 'said' in order to indicate that there need not be anything specifically linguistic about the act for these features to be present. Even in the act of correcting a child's movement by putting a limb, say, in a certain position, the child's attention has been drawn to something together with something about it. The same applies to the other forms of communication that I have mentioned. Thus, as I suggested in chapter 6, there may be something propositional about the child's thought when these communicative acts are understood even before he knows anything of language proper. There is at any rate nothing wrong with describing the child as recognising that .... . Moreover, if we ask how the child can come to understand the notions that are presupposed by the propositional style of description of his thought, how, that is, he can come to distinguish between what the thought is about and what is thought about it, it is reasonable to point to the general features of those communicative acts that go on almost from the beginning.

It may be objected that this again is not sufficient to explain how it actually happens. Surely the child has to receive a communication, of whatever form, *as* a communication. How can it do this if it has no idea of what a communication is, and how therefore can it get that idea? This objection has much in common with the one that I considered in the last chapter about the child's coming to accept correction *as* correction. How can it do this if it does not already know what correction is? To deal with the problem one has to look in the same direction. Acts of communication are carried out by and come from persons, or at any rate certainly not from mere things. A natural emotional response to treatment in kind, something that I suggested lies at the basis of the personal relationships on which other developments as a human being depend, is in one sense a communicative act, a communication of feeling. By itself it would be little more than that, and this would be compatible with the description of it as a mere suggestion or even infection of feeling, the kind of thing that goes on when a mood is caught or when an infectious feeling passes from one person to another. One might explain the phenomenon in strictly causal terms. To treat another person, however, in a certain way, say a loving one, and to get a response of similar or different kind in return, need not be just this. To suppose that it must be is to forget the context in which such interchanges of treatment and response go on. Such interchange may be founded on natural reactions, which may conceivably be construable in a causal way, but they are not themselves purely causal in that way. We must see that the child comes in the course of a whole mass of behaviour of this kind to recognise certain sources of behaviour as persons, in a gradually developing way.

Hence the child comes to interchange reactions and attitudes—in effect to communicate—without initially or necessarily recognising that this is what it is engaged in. With, however, a growing consciousness, along the lines suggested in the last chapter, an awareness of communication as an aim and not just a natural activity to engage in is likely to emerge. All this of course presupposes the community of wants, ends and feelings that I spoke of in chapter 6. The child becomes progressively initiated into forms of life that those around it engage in and follow out continually; and this is possible because the child, as a result of its natural constitution, is a potential sharer in these forms of life and needs to be made an actual sharer in ,them by being constantly treated as one. In a word, the child comes to communicate by being communicated with. There are of course limits to this, as with all forms of treatment of the very young. A child cannot be treated as an adult, if adequate development is to result, not even as an adult *manqué*; but for this purpose he cannot be treated, on the other hand, as something that has no connection with adult, human ways of behaving. It is in a way fortunate that parents do not usually have too sophisticated a view of infants; for it is the treatment of them as, in large part, small and undeveloped human beings that makes them, or helps to make them, larger and more developed participants of the same community.

I have argued, then, that the child gets the idea of communication by being communicated with, as it were. I have also argued that there can be something propositional about the child's thought even before it is capable of uttering and using actual propositions, and indeed that this must be so if the child is to have thought in any genuine sense. Moreover, this thought is encouraged and, as it were, drawn out, by the fact that the treatment that it receives from adults has certain features which in a way correspond to some at least of the structural elements in language. I wish now to elaborate this point, since all that I have said so far is that one can find in certain acts features corresponding to that of drawing attention to something in a way that allows something to be communicated about what is so picked out. To be content with that would not get us very far into language; it would provide us with the basic features of reference and description, but nothing else. What else that is in some sense linguistic or analogous to what is linguistic can one find in human action, behavioural interchange and mutual emotional expression? The answer is 'a very great deal', for human behaviour and what it expresses is saturated with that which is propositionally styled. That is to say that, just as thought can be said to have a propositional flavour even when distinct propositional elements cannot be distinguished in the formulation of the thought itself, so actions can be said to have an analogous propositional flavour. Indeed, something would not count as an action if it did not have this.

What I mean is the following; it is of a part with the claim often made by philosophers that actions are imbued with meaning. Action emerges, as I have tried to indicate, from what is not action proper, but mere reaction, which can conceivably be explained in strictly causal terms. One comes eventually to do things because one has seen a situation in a certain way, *as* such and such, or because one wants something or other, or because that is what one is intending to do. These uses of 'because' are not strictly causal in the sense appropriate to mere reaction. Suppose that one sees something as threatening or disturbing and acts accordingly. Someone else seeing the action or course of behaviour, without necessarily seeing the situation for what it is, might say, 'He is acting as if there were something threatening or disturbing.' The action is of a kind that is appropriate to a situation seen in that way. To say this is, of course, not to say that any fully propositional thought has passed through the mind of the person referred to, to the effect that the situation is of the kind that it is supposed to be. It cannot validly be maintained that an action is always backed, if it is to be of a certain kind, by a fully propositional thought of an appropriate kind. Nevertheless, the action may be a kind of embodiment of such a thought, to the extent that it is an appropriate response to a situation if that situation is construed in a certain way.

That is most obvious, of course, where the action is the expression of a belief or of knowledge; for in that case the action can certainly be described, and indeed must be so, in terms that bring in that belief or knowledge, and it must be construed in such a way that it is of this kind for the person who so acts. That is because when the act is an expression of such a belief or knowledge it is likely to be fully intentional; and even if it is not true that every intentional act is itself an expression of intention in the sense that it can be construed as arising from an explicit thought of the form 'I shall do ...', it must nevertheless be performed under a certain description. This implies that, if it is to be so performed, the person concerned must be at least capable of recognising *that* the act is of the kind that it is, and *that* the circumstances in which it is to be performed are of the kind that they are or are taken to be. Even where an action is not fully intentional (or of course unintentional) it is likely to be subject to what Elizabeth Anscombe has called a 'mental cause', e.g., where someone jumps because of a bang. In such cases we construe what takes place in terms of something that makes reference (although not always explicitly) to what takes place in the person's mind: in the case mentioned by way of example his hearing the sound, his hearing *that* there was a big bang. Thus in such cases there will be a propositionally construable mental occurrence related to the act, even if we cannot say that the act is the intentional expression of it. We can construe the act as a 'jump' (rather than, say, a muscular spasm) only if it originates from and can be seen as playing a part in the life of someone who can take things as such and such, recognise them as such and such, and so on.

Thus when someone makes a threatening gesture towards me, it is not only the case that I may recognise that the person has a certain intention, not only the case that I may recognise that I am being put in a certain position; it is also that I may recognise the maker of the gesture as construing the situation in a certain way and making a demand on me that has a kind of imperatival force. Analogously I might construe another kind of gesture not only as one made by a person who has a certain view of the situation but also as the expression of a wish, as the expression of 'if only I were …'. In each of these cases I can of course be mistaken, but an understanding of other people's behaviour requires that there should be these possibilities at least. One who makes a certain hopeless gesture which we construe as an expression of 'if only …' has not necessarily had a thought in these explicit terms, but it is not enough to say that all that matters is that *we* construe it in these terms; it has to have something of this significance for him too.

I have no idea of exactly when an understanding of the grammatical construction 'if only …' is likely to be acquired by a child; nor do I know what the probable order is for the acquisition of the understanding of various grammatical constructions. It is quite possible that our intuitions about such things might be wrong. I think, however, that it is abundantly clear that the acquisition of such understanding must be seen against the background of forms of behaviour which are a natural focus for what is the characteristic use of such grammatical constructions.

To put the matter in terms of the competence/performance distinction which Chomsky makes so much of, acquisition of a certain linguistic competence must be seen against the background of the natural or characteristic contexts for its performance. It is a mistake to suppose that the acquisition of a piece of linguistic competence is to be construed as like the acquisition of a skill or knack that may be isolated from all the background behaviour and understanding of the learner. Learning the use of a construction like 'if only ...' is not like learning to wiggle one's ears.

What much of this comes to is the thesis that something cannot properly be said to act or behave in a human sense if it cannot see *that* things are such and such, if it cannot believe or know things, and so on. Whether or not physical action is identical with or construable as identical with bodily movement *simpliciter*, that which so acts cannot be construed simply as the source of such bodily movement. To see something as engaging in action we must see it as much else; *a fortiori*, to see something as an action of a certain kind is a very complex matter. Since understanding is, as I have emphasised throughout, a matter of degree, it is right to expect that anything more than a very low degree of understanding of action will take time to come about. In the first two years of life a child has an immense amount to learn, but it is clear that he or she will have a very considerable understanding of the immediate world and the people in it, together with the relations between them and him or her, by the time that even the beginnings of understanding of language are manifested in a recognisable way. The further understanding that language itself brings must emerge out of what already exists as a result of the general forms of intercourse that the child has had with others, particularly the adults in its environment.

What then does language bring that was not there before? Piaget, as I have already noted, claims that language emerges out of 'symbolic functions', and on this picture of it language is just a more abstract and complex form of symbolisation than other uses of symbols involve. It is no doubt true that before the explicit use of language has manifested itself the child has gained some understanding of, and perhaps use of, symbols. While it is wrong to look on language as just a more abstract set of symbols than others (for this would exclude the structural, grammatical aspects of language and the complex functions that the grammatical aspects fulfil), it remains true that it *is* more abstract than other symbols. There is little that is iconic, for example, about language. The understanding of the use of a word and of the grammatical and other contexts of its use has at its back a whole mass of other knowledge and understanding which the word somehow sums up by providing a focus for it without its having to be made explicit. To have learnt the word 'Daddy' is not simply to have learnt that that word goes with a particular person or even a particular kind of person. As I noted in chapter 6, Vygotsky claims that the first word uttered by a child amounts to a whole sentence. What sentence, however, does the use of the word 'Daddy' correspond to and amount to? There could be no clear answer to that question. Imitation no doubt plays a great part in what the child does in its earliest years, and it might even be the case that certain words are used first because they are put before the child's attention most directly and most frequently. It might also be the case that some words are used because the child likes the sound of them or because their use and utterance receives encouragement from parents. And so on. My point is that there can be no definite answer to the question of why a given word is *uttered* first. If, however, it is used as a word, as a speech element in a genuine act of communication, then what Vygotsky says may be right. Nevertheless, it cannot even so be said what sentence the word amounts to. The use of the word brings to a focus a whole web of understanding that the child has acquired, but in what way that understanding is being expressed it is impossible to say. It need hardly be said that the child cannot tell us!

One answer that will not do here is that the child has learnt father's name and is giving it as a sign of recognition when father comes in. A few sentences ago I said that to have learnt the word 'Daddy' is not simply to have learnt that that word goes with a particular person. I was being deliberately indefinite in using the words 'goes with'. It is clear enough that *if* a child uses the word 'Daddy' when recognising his father he has learnt that the word does in some sense go with that person; I was casting doubt both on the supposition that this could be said without the satisfaction of the condition mentioned and on the claim that this is in any case all that the child has come to learn. What I am now concerned with is the much more precise claim that the child has learnt a person's name. Accounts of the origins of language have often supposed that the rest of language somehow emerges out of a primitive understanding of names (although others have often suggested that the origins of language might be expected to be connected with more practical concerns). Wittgenstein has taught us, however, that naming and the use of names is just one function of language, and cannot be understood except as an aspect, and just one aspect at that, of the use of language. To understand that a certain word is something's name presupposes an understanding of one linguistic use in isolation from others; it also presupposes an understanding of that conventional form of behaviour which is involved in giving something a name and treating that word thereafter as the thing's name, however else one speaks of that thing. It is not likely that someone could understand a word as a name until he had already acquired some use of language in general and perhaps had reflected to some extent on the circumstances of that use. If it is natural, for people who are concerned with the use of language and how by its means we manage to communicate things about the world to others, to seize upon the use of names as in some sense primitive, that does not mean that the use and understanding of names *is* primitive in language learning.

If, therefore, we agree that when the child first uses 'Daddy' as a word, he is trying to say something and that to that extent the word amounts to a sentence (the unit of *saying*), we cannot justifiably assume that the sentence is equivalent to anything like 'That's Daddy', or to any sentence in which the word 'Daddy' functions as a definite name. We cannot say what the sentence in question must be; only that the child is trying to say something and that this word somehow serves as the focus of what he is trying to say. Moreover, what he is trying to say cannot even be clear to the child himself, since he does not as yet have the means of making it clear to himself. Hence the word amounts to a sentence that is inchoate in the sense that it is unformed and cannot as yet be given form, but which for the child somehow focuses that very considerable understanding that he has in relation to the person who is his father. Hence, if we ask what the word means for the child we can answer only that it means all that. As language-use grows and becomes more complicated so will the ways in which that background knowledge and understanding are applied and focused in the use of words become complicated also; so that eventually we cannot even say all or even much of what a word means for us in that sense.

What any symbol does for us is thus what I suggested earlier: it serves as the focus for a whole mass of understanding which because of it does not have to be made explicit. Without what Piaget calls the 'symbolic function', that understanding and knowledge would have to be made explicit if it were to be used at all, and this would in effect make it impossible for it to be used for any thinking that was at all abstract. That is to say that it would make impossible any thinking that presupposed a body of knowledge or understanding which is divorced from the circumstances in which it ordinarily gets application for the person or animal concerned. Without the symbol that knowledge and its circumstances would have to be made explicit, and this would prevent one from considering new applications for it. A further point in this connection is that once the question of the application of something arises, there arises also thereby the possibility of misapplication of it, so that questions of getting it right or wrong become pertinent. Hence the use of symbols brings with it those very possibilities, and an understanding of symbols an understanding of those possibilities. On the other hand, an understanding of this is hardly enough for an understanding of *linguistic* possibilities. Even granted the point that the symbol provides the focus for a body of implicit knowledge which can be applied or misapplied, this tells us nothing of the *ways* in which it can be applied and how it functions as part of the activity of saying something. Nor would the understanding of a symbol be, on the account so far given, an understanding of what might be said. It would probably be going too far to say that something cannot count as a symbol except in the context of saying something or of something's being said (a religious symbol may, for example, function in terms of its emotional significance, although even here it is difficult to think of its doing merely that). On the other hand it does seem plausible to say that something's functioning as a symbol presupposes a background of propositionally styled thought or actions which have the propositional flavour that I referred to earlier. In other words, something may function as a symbol for a person or animal only if it has a place in some course of thought or action on its part which may be said to be propositionally styled.

I said in chapter 6, when considering the possibilities of animal thought and understanding, that we can apply such notions to animals only to the extent that we can think of them as having something like the concepts of truth and falsity. That idea gets application here too. One might say that what makes a form of understanding linguistic or something that is linguistically coloured is, among other things, that it involves an understanding of truth and falsity in the definite form that these notions have in application to sayings. Thus the child's learning of language is the learning of an institution which has these ideas at its centre. Indeed, it has sometimes been said by philosophers of language that it is important for language learning that the adults with whom the child grows up should in general say what is true. I am not sure that the matter is best put in that way. Certainly the child has to catch on to the idea that one of the functions of language is truth-telling, that an understanding of what is said presupposes that that is so, and that while anything that is said may be up for assessment as true or false it is truth that is the norm. An understanding that truth is the norm does not, however, necessarily demand for its acquisition that people in the child's environment should generally, i.e. statistically most often, tell the truth. The supposal that it does imply this presupposes, I suggest, a certain conception of what learning consists of: the implanting of an idea through the frequency of its presentation, a conception that assimilates learning to something akin to conditioning and is part of the empiricist view that I reviewed in chapter 2.

Certainly the child has to catch on to the ideas of truth and falsity and to the idea of truth as the norm, but that does not necessarily imply any definite view about how the learning goes on. I have repeatedly laid weight in earlier chapters on the notion of correction in this connection. The child's learning of the different constituents of language and their meaning takes place, as we have seen, in the context of a general understanding, partial but growing, of what people are and do, and of what the activity of language-use is in particular. This is all part of the general commerce of interpersonal relations within which children are brought up. To suppose that a child has to be confronted with a generality of true statements in order to understand what truth, and thereby language-use in general, are is to forget the wider context from which language-use emerges: a context of varying activity, pre-linguistic communication, and the relationships with others that this presupposes. Moreover, while truth-telling is no doubt the central function of language, there are other ways in which language fits into the background of which I have spoken. It may be used to draw attention to things, to get things done, to express wishes, etc. It is nevertheless arguable that, as I have said, none of these would count as uses of *language* if language were not usable for saying things in a way that is up for assessment as true or false. Thus the child's learning of language is in a genuine sense an initiation into an institution, a way of going on governed by rules, aims and procedures which are public in the sense that they are common and shared by others. Even without the specific arguments that Chomsky invokes for the thesis, it is reasonable to hold with him that the learning of language is a two-tiered business, whether or not the tiers are surmounted in succession.

There is first the learning of the general functions of language and all that this brings with it: what talking is as distinct from making mere noises on the one hand and non-linguistic communication on the other. This embraces such apparently different things as grammatical structure, meaning and truth. The grammatical structure with which we are here concerned is that at the level that Chomsky calls deep structure; however it is represented in the saying, it makes such possible such distinctions as that between the subject of what is said and what is said about it. Without this kind of complexity, which may or may not be evident at the level of surface structure, the noises emitted or received are not up for categorisation as sayings. Grammatical structure is not all, however, that there is to it; there are also the semantic aspects, the fact that what is said and thereby indeed the elements of what is said have meaning; this implies that the symbols function according to publically accepted rules which have to be learnt in one way or another. Neither the syntactical or grammatical features nor the semantic ones, however, would either together or separately be enough without the recognition that within a context of communication the sayings have to serve functions, the chief and paramount case of which is said to be fulfilled when it is said that the saying is true. It was Frege's insight that only in the context of a proposition does a word have meaning, and this remark brings together the factors that I have mentioned. In independence of propositions (sayings) the notion of the meaning of a word is merely an abstraction; a proposition has structure, a structure which in some way reflects what is essential to a saying; and a proposition is that which is either true or false. Nevertheless, a proposition is itself an abstraction from the life of a language, since language is, as Wittgenstein insisted, a form of life, a human institution and an essential part of human activity in a context which must be described as social. A child's learning of the fundamentals of language is an initiation into all this.

The other tier is represented by the form that the actual language learnt by the individual takes and by the matter of which it is constituted. That is what Chomsky has called the surface structure of language, and it can be learnt, only if given knowledge of the deep structure. That 'only if given', however, should be interpreted in a logical sense. There is no necessity that the child should learn or even know independently of learning, that deep structure before he can learn the form and matter that an actual language, such as English, takes. It is possible to learn the one in learning the other, although they both have their foundations in much that goes on in pre-linguistic life. It is not my intention in this chapter to give a thorough account of language learning. Such an account would in any case require a knowledge of a whole host of empirical facts that I do not have at my disposal, and which may not even be known at all in many cases. As in other aspects of learning a philosopher's job is not to usurp the empirical role that others may fulfil. The philosopher's account should be an answer to the question 'How are we to understand its possibility?'. In setting out the preconditions of language and of the context of its acquisition I have tried to say something to that effect. No doubt there is an immense amount to say in addition to this, but as far as I am concerned it must rest there.

9   Later learning

A distinction between early and later learning was made by D. O. Hebb in his *The Organization of Behaviour* (1949) against the background of the controversy then existing between those who thought of learning as a continuous process through which stimulus-response connections are built up and those who thought that there must be discontinuities where insight dawns or jumps of thought are made. It would not be profitable to go into that controversy here, since its terms of reference were very much the behaviourist psychology of the period. That there should be a difference, however, between the learning processes at the beginning of a child's life (or, for that matter, an animal's) and those that characteristically take place later is very much what we should expect. Hebb suggested that early learning was a slow, continuous business and on the whole concerned with generalities, while later learning was quick and often punctuated by jumps in which the learner leaps from one thing to another. As far as human learning is concerned we might expect there to be initially a slow building up of concepts in the course of a gradual process in which things are distinguished and sorted out. This might very well be characterised as a process of particularisation, so that what is first seen in general terms is gradually given specificity. I say 'might very well be characterised' since the actual course of learning may be very various, depending on the circumstances in which the learner finds himself, particularly the circumstances provided by other people. Nevertheless, one would expect things to be seen in terms of broad similarities first, so that to speak of the process as one of particularisation would not be an unfair description of its trend. Later learning will involve the use of concepts already acquired, and their extension and modification in the face of increasing experience. The similarities and distinctions perceived may then be of a quite different character from what was the case earlier, and the leaps of thought and insight more frequent. Hence learning would be expected to take place more quickly when it occurs. This seems to be a fair general picture of the situation.

It is only one picture, however, and it might be thought that

Piaget's picture of the situation as represented by his account of the different stages of intellectual development is a rival. According to Piaget, as we saw in chapter 4, the earliest stage is that in which development takes place mainly in the sensori-motor field. This is followed by the pre-operational sub-stage and the stage of concrete operations generally, and there is finally the stage of formal operations. Could not this be described as representing a move from the particular to the general, and thus one that proceeds in the opposite direction to the one that I previously described? Piaget himself describes the process that he outlines as one of progressive decentration. I shall not repeat here the arguments that I surveyed in chapter 4. For present purposes the main thing to indicate is that there is no real conflict between the two pictures of the course of learning that I have mentioned. In the first place, the early-later learning distinction is a very rough one, and there need be no claim that it covers the whole range covered by Piaget's three stages. Second, the general-particular distinction is not strictly commensurate with the formal or abstract-concrete distinction.[1] One might represent Piaget's account as one according to which there is a progressive throwing off of the chains of perception and bodily action (there are analogies here with Plato's theory of education as given in the *Republic*, although there are of course differences too). During the sensori-motor stage there is a preoccupation with finding one's way about the world in a physical sense; during the period of concrete operations the intellect is still confined by the conditions that attention to perceptual factors imposes; it is only in the final stage that intellectual operations of a completely abstract kind become possible.

If thought is abstract and formal, it is of course concerned in a certain sense with what is general, since formal relations hold in virtue of the logical characteristics of general features. Where X is the reciprocal of Y (to take one of the elements of Piaget's INRC grouping referred to in chapter 4), there is a formal operation by means of which X can be transformed into Y, irrespective of the precise values of X and Y. One might say that in this case X and Y stand equally poised round a centre (as in the numerical notion of reciprocity where the reciprocals are symmetrically related to the number 1, so that one of them can be transformed into the other by repeating a second time whatever operation will take one of them to 1). Such relations would not be possible unless the terms of the relation had a certain generality, such that what holds between them can hold between all other terms of the same type. That is to say that it must make sense to use the expression 'of the same type' in connection with them, and the notion of type implies generality. Nevertheless, generality and abstractness are not the same notions. It is possible to think generally about the world without that thought having an abstract character; one might indeed say that to think really generally about the world may be to think about it in a way that lacks real content, but is nevertheless to think about *it*. To think abstractly implies a certain detachment from things, a certain preoccupation with concepts for their own sake in isolation from the conditions of their application to things. Within abstractness there may be degrees of generality and specificity. What Piaget provides is in fact a picture of what is *possible* for the intellect: a trend towards greater abstractness and attention to formal considerations. Whether or not people do use their intellect in that way depends on all sorts of other factors. I do not say that this is in fact the way that Piaget looks at the issues, but it seems to be a reasonable way to look at them, and it has something to do with what he says.

If one views the matter in terms of structures, as Piaget does, it is possible to say that generality-specificity is a dimension of the structures which is concerned with their scope and comprehensiveness. One structure is more general than another to the extent that it covers a wider range of phenomena and to the extent that it takes in less of the detail of what it structures. The abstractness of a structure is not a matter of this but of its lack of concern with any of the concrete features of what it structures. If we could think of the development of a view of the world as a process of structuring and restructuring, the generality of the structures would be reflected in their scope; their abstractness would be reflected in their detachment from concrete circumstances. To that extent, if we could think of structures of differing orders (structures, structures of structures, and so on) we should then be concerned with degrees of abstractness, and this would not necessarily be commensurate with generality in any straightforward sense.

Given all this, it should be clear that the two pictures of the learning process which I have mentioned are not incompatible, since they are concerned with different things: Hebb's picture being concerned with the differences between the main characteristics of early learning and those of what may take place later, Piaget's picture being concerned with the increasing possibilities open to the intellect, and therefore with what we may expect as regards intellectual processes at any given stage of life. It is important to see it in this latter way. It is not that all children at a certain age think in a given way, or rather that is not how Piaget ought to represent the matter; it is rather that if they have been through certain previous stages it is open to them to think in this way; and it is not possible for them to do so if they have not, or so Piaget claims. I add that note of scepticism for what must by now be the familiar reason that while it is clear that there must be, as mentioned in chapter 4, what Toulmin has called conceptual stratification if certain concepts presuppose others, logically if not temporally, it does not follow from that consideration that there must be the general ordering of intellectual possibilities that the theory of stages implies. That is to say that it does not follow that there can be no sign of, say, formal and abstract thought until a whole period of concrete operations has been passed through. Given what human beings are and what human experience is like it would be impossible to think of abstract thought preceding concrete thought altogether.[2] There is nothing in this, however, that prevents the possibility of a certain degree of abstract thought manifesting itself at a comparatively early age, if only as an isolated phenomenon and in an isolated area. If the Piagetian stages are valid they are so only if construed as a necessary sequence of general tendencies; that is to say that it may be a valid thesis that the general tendency to think abstractly must necessarily be preceded by a tendency of a more concrete sort. Even so, that may not be the right way to put it. It might be better to say that the *possibility* of thinking abstractly in general must necessarily be preceded by a stage at which in general only the possibility of concrete thought exists.

I shall not go further into these considerations. It is reasonable to think that the progressive interrelationships between experience and understanding may lead to an increasing ability to think in a way relatively independent of experience, and even to revise one's view of experience in terms of that way of thinking. Whether it is for the same reason right to think of the growth of understanding as a progressive process of decentration, a move away from egocentricity, depends on what is the correct view of experience and its relation to understanding. Piaget undoubtedly views experience, at any rate as it is initially, as something private and personal. There is, however, an ambiguity to be noted here. Perception does, of course, involve a point of view or perspective; one cannot *but* see things from a point of view. That does not entail that what one may come to know through perception must be in any pejorative sense egocentric. Nor does it imply that one cannot come to be able to put oneself in another's position and thereby come to know how things are from his point of view. To do this, however, requires imagination and a certain intelligence.

Some of the Piagetian investigations into the moves away from egocentricity seem to be concerned with just that: they are investigations into the possibilities of children adopting points of view which are other than their own, and are therefore investigations into the use of imagination and intelligent understanding.

To say that perception necessarily involves a point of view is not, however, to say that there is an initial privacy about the experience from which the individual has somehow to move into a public world. It is not, that is, that the child has an initial awareness only of what is private to him; I have indicated the wrongness of such a view in chapter 7. I tried to indicate there and in earlier chapters that a child's experience must be construed as an experience of a common world from the beginning, though not of course initially of this *as* a common world. It is to this that the child has to come, but there would be no possibility of doing so if the experience were necessarily concerned with private objects at first. It is only because the situation is other than this that a child can come to distinguish right and wrong ways of seeing things. Egocentricity cannot, therefore, be regarded as tantamount to privacy or subjectivity; if it is to be looked on as a defect by comparison with adult attitudes (and it is by no means obvious that 'defect' is the right word), it is one due to an insufficiently educated imagination, a failure to see things from points of view other than one's own immediate one. This is a failure that can exist only where other points of view are possible; it can be remarked on only because it constitutes a deviation from a norm. In other words, the egocentricity of the young child, to the extent that it exists, is simply one facet of the growth of an understanding of a public world, a facet that is due to the fact that people necessarily have points of view. It is not a general characteristic of experience itself. Indeed Vygotsky has claimed that it must *succeed* an initial socialisation as an internalisation of what is until then external. This is in effect to say that a private and personal point of view is possible only if given an awareness of what is public and inter-subjective. The view has some plausibility.

What I have said so far has been concerned with the increased possibilities of understanding that may come about with increased experience. I have been concerned merely to indicate something of the framework for those possibilities. How and whether the possibilities are realised will depend on many factors other than those which I have mentioned, not all of which need bear on solely intellectual considerations. There are also emotional and other motivational considerations, for example. There are, moreover, social considerations which may affect the kind of environment in which the individual grows up and lives, and the opportunities that this affords or stunts. There are no doubt other considerations that arise from the individual's own make-up, his character, personality and temperament. It would be foolish to think that it must be possible to give an account of the typical course of development of a human being. If it is possible to say something about the framework of possibilities that I have mentioned it is because the issues are conceptual, not straightforwardly empirical. They arise from questions of the form 'How is it possible that ... ?' One might ask, for example, how, given that mature understanding of the world is of a certain kind and that experience is to be construed in a certain way, it is possible for that understanding to come about on the basis of experience. A question of that form is one that is typically philosophical.

Having said, however, the kind of thing that I have said in earlier chapters concerning the way in which increased understanding of the world comes about through a kind of interplay between perceptual experience and the kind of knowledge or understanding involved in having concepts, granted certain background conditions, there is little left for the philosopher, *qua* philosopher, to say. The details of how it actually takes place in given individuals or perhaps given sets of individuals must be left to the empirical investigator. The only *general* answer that is possible to the questions 'How do people learn things?' and 'How do people acquire an understanding of things, how do they acquire concepts?' is 'In all sorts of ways'. It all depends on who and where they are, and where they start from in the learning process. It is certainly not enough, for example, if a person is to acquire a given concept, that he should be presented with a wide range of relevant experiences, unless he is in the position to see them as relevant. That will depend on, among other things, what he takes the experiences *as*, what they mean to him and whether, for a variety of reasons, not all of which are intellectual, they are capable of meaning anything to him.

That means that, apart from the increased possibilities of understanding that I have referred to so far, one can speak also of increased possibilities of experience itself. There is a sense in which we can say of some people that they are incapable of experiencing some thing, or of others that their lives have given them a wide or deep experience of certain things or indeed quite generally. We can learn to experience things in certain ways where we have not done so before. This is a point of some importance, because the account that I have given so far may suggest that learning is always and simply a matter of gaining fresh knowledge and understanding. We can, however, learn to see things in new ways, we can learn to attach significance to things in a variety of ways, not all of which can be said, strictly speaking, to be a matter of understanding or knowing them. Thus while understanding may be involved in learning to have an aesthetic appreciation of something, we are not in learning to have that aesthetic appreciation necessarily coming to understand the object as such. It may simply be a matter of coming to see things about it that we have not previously seen. A failure to see something in a certain way may involve a lack of sensitivity, and sometimes such a lack of sensitivity may be due to something in our natural constitution. But not always. It may be because we have not learnt to use that natural constitution, in not having learnt, for example, to use our eyes properly. At other times it may be because we have not learnt to look at things from the right point of view or to attend to the right features of them. It may be that we have not learnt to connect the understanding that we do have with experience so as to see things under given concepts. While such learning does not have knowledge or understanding of things as its end, it does involve these in one way or another and it does involve the acquisition of know-how. Much learning is, of course, learning how to do things and thus involves the acquisition of skill. Many skills presuppose in their performance building on to and putting to use things that are not themselves performances, e.g., habits, natural reactions, and equally passive experiences. There is a clear sense in which an ability to see something in a certain way may be in this way a form of skill and can accordingly be acquired through learning.

I do not mean to suggest by this that on *every* occasion on which we might say of someone that he has learnt to see something in a certain way (particularly where seeing it in this way involves attaching a significance of some kind to it) we should be right to say that he had acquired a skill of some kind. Apart from anything else, that might suggest simply that there was a kind of cleverness about his viewpoint. When a man says, for example, that he has learnt through long experience to see a certain organisation as sinister, he is not just clever at seeing it in that way, even if coming to see it in that way may have involved know-how on his part. He may be able to point to features of the organisation which suggest to him that that is how it ought to be seen, and those features, when pointed out, may or may not enable others to see it in the same way. All that he means is that he has come through experience to see it in that way, *and* that his seeing it in that way is grounded in experience, not merely caused by it. The part that follows the '*and*' is important. Where seeing something in a certain way is caused by experience simply, we may say 'Something in my experience has made me see it in that way, so that I just do'; we do not say 'I have learnt to see it in that way'. There is equally a difference between 'I have learnt to love her' and 'I have come to love her', let alone 'Something in my experience made me love her'. When I said that for learning the way of seeing must be *grounded* in experience the implication was that experience had suggested that this was the right way to see it. There is something of the same suggestion in 'I have learnt to love her'. Although there may be a technique involved, that is not all that there is to it, and to concentrate on that might well give the impression that it was all a bit of a trick, perhaps even a deceit. Just as learning that p implies that the acceptance of p is grounded in experience, so learning to do something in certain circumstances (or learning to see something in a certain way or to feel something of a certain kind) implies that that is in some sense the right thing to do, in that it fits in with one's experience.

One cannot, however, lay down in advance what course experience must take if one is to learn some fact or learn to do something; nor can we rule out in advance the possibilities that any given course of experience may provide in this connection. This is particularly clear in such cases as learning to love someone; the experience that may be the basis of this in one person's case may be very surprising to others. What is requisite, however, is that the experience should indeed be a basis for and not merely the cause of the final state. That is to say that the person who has learnt must in principle, although not necessarily of course in fact, be able to say what is the relevance of the experience to the final state. There must be a story to tell, which is one that is more than a reference to a cause *simpliciter*, whether or not the person concerned can actually tell it. It has often been maintained by philosophers in recent times that attitudes and emotions (perhaps as distinct from moods) involve beliefs or judgments. A man can properly be said to feel pride in something only if he believes that the thing in question is valuable or praiseworthy and only if he believes that he has some kind of responsibility for it. It may be too strong to speak of 'belief' and 'judgment' in this connection, at any rate in some cases; it remains true that the person concerned must see whatever it is in these ways. A man may justifiably take pride in his achievements, but if he has learnt to loathe them it must be because he has learnt to see them differently, perhaps as worthless and not achievements at all. On the other hand, if he simply comes to loathe them it may be for quite different reasons; in such circumstances he no doubt sees what he formerly regarded as achievements quite differently, but he may have just come to see them in this new way without there being any considerations that are relevant to his so doing, except causally. That would mark the difference between learning to do something and merely coming to do it. It is clear, however, that the issues over learning to have a certain attitude or emotion towards something turn on analogous issues over learning to see things in certain ways, since the relevant factor in the emotion is the seeing of the thing in a certain way; we can, therefore, confine our attention to that for present purposes.

What determines whether the final state is grounded in experi-ence, as I have said that it must be if that state is to be one of hav-ing learnt, or whether it is caused by that experience? It has to be admitted that it may be very difficult to determine this in parti-cular cases, and it may be impossible to give a general account which will help to provide such a determination in particular cases. That is why it is so tempting to say that one could not learn, e.g., to play golf by standing on one's head;³ it is tempting because it looks in such a case as if there could be nothing relevant to golf in such an activity (and it might seem even more obvious that something of the sort is the case in other instances of learning). If one is seduced by this temptation it is likely that one will be inclined to insist that if the knowledge of how to play golf did come about by such means it could only be a case in which the knowledge is produced causally, even if in a very surprising way. It might, however, be a mistake to set bounds on the possible connections that may exist for some people between apparently different activities or situations. For this reason I think that the temptation of which I have spoken should be resisted. Doing so does not, however, make the distinction that we are seeking to establish any easier to make. Moreover, the situation may be complicated if one admits, as perhaps one should do, along with some contemporary philosophers,⁴ that it is only causation that makes a reason, consideration or ground efficacious as far as action and perhaps other states of a person are concerned. That is to say that, even in those cases where the final state is grounded in experience rather than simply caused by it, causality must come into the picture somewhere if the grounding is to be efficacious.

We may gain some help in attempting to deal with this problem by going back to some of the issues discussed in chapter 5. In effect I tried to show there that the more a perceptual situation has to do with sensation and the purely sensory the more it becomes appropriate to speak of causality, since sensations and what produces them constitute some of the causal conditions under which perception takes place. Thus, to the extent that an illusion, for example, can be classified as sensory, to that extent it seems pertinent to look for causal factors in its explanation, causal factors which lie behind its purely sensory aspects and which may therefore be held responsible for the sensations that we have when we perceive the object in this way. If the Müller-Lyer illusion, for example, *is* a sensory illusion, we might look for its explanation in the way that the arrow-heads on the parallel and equal-length lines brings about a sensory experience different from the one that we should have without them; we should not look for the explanation, on the supposition in question, in any features of our understanding or in our beliefs. It would in that case scarcely make sense to say that we have learnt to see the lines in this way, even though our understanding enters the picture to the extent that we could not see the lines as unequal unless we understood what it was for lines to be or look unequal.

On the other hand, we might well learn to see them as *equal* despite the things that pull us towards seeing them as unequal; we might, that is, acquire a technique for confining our attention to the lines in such a way as to ignore the arrow-heads, so overcoming the things that might otherwise cause us to see the lines as unequal. Likewise, in the case of ambiguous figures, we might acquire a technique for seeing them in certain ways at will, perhaps by attending to certain features of the figures rather than others; some people might not be able to acquire that technique and would in that case be dependent on the way that the figure takes them. Sometimes there may be an oscillation in the look of the figure in a way that people cannot control; the explanation of this may lie in a vacillation of attention, so that the reason why those people see the figure in a given way at a given time may lie in something about them as well as in something about the figure. It will then be true of those people that they have not learnt to see the figure in a given way, but that if they do come to see it in that way there is something of the kind mentioned that causes them to do so.

In the cases that I have mentioned, where we do learn to see whatever it is in a certain way it is because we have acquired a technique to that end; and such a situation is clearly distinguished from the situations in which we just come to see it in that way by the presence or absence of a technique. These cases do not, however, distinguish learning to see *that* something is so from merely coming to see that it is so. In each case, though in different ways, there is an alternative way of seeing possible, and what is learned is a technique for seeing the thing in one way at will. Hence it might be objected that what has been distinguished is learning to be *able to see* the thing in a certain way as distinct from simply coming to be so able, or perhaps from coming simply to do so. Nevertheless, we can adapt the cases that I have mentioned or similar ones to bring about what we need. In the case of the ambiguous figures it might be that someone initially saw them in one way without knowing that they had an alternative aspect; and he might come subsequently to see that they had the other aspect. In that case there would be no suggestion that the person in question could see the figures in one way or the other at will. His coming to see the alternative aspect might be inexplicable except in terms such as that something caught his attention and the aspect in question dawned upon him; there would be no suggestion of his having learnt anything in this. There might be a similar situation with regard to the Müller-Lyer illusion. While this is not an ambiguous figure in a strict sense it does admit of being seen either in an illusory way or in a veridical way. Given that is is natural to see the lines as of unequal length, someone might initially see them only in that way and subsequently come to see that they were really of the same length. There might be some kind of causal explanation for this too, and in such circumstances we could hardly say that he had learnt to see that the lines were of equal length. We might, however, say that he had *learnt that* the lines were of equal length. This may seem a subtle distinction. The point is that in seeing the lines in this way, however this has come about, he will probably have acquired knowledge about the actual nature of the lines, and there is a sense of 'learn' in which simply to acquire knowledge or information about something from experience is to learn about it. In that case he will have acquired this information about the real length of the lines through seeing them in this way; and so he has learnt how the lines actually are. That, however, does not entail that he has also learnt to *see* the lines as of this kind.

How *could* he do this? The answer that I gave earlier was that it would be correct to say that he had done this if he came to see that the lines were of this kind and his so seeing them was grounded in experience (*not*, given what was said earlier, 'came to be *able* to see them in this way', which would be a different thing). One way in which this might come about would be if he were to attend to the larger context and see the lines as part of a larger pattern, so seeing as well the way in which the arrow-heads functioned in his experience. In that way he would come not merely to know that the lines were of equal length but to see this as well. It is not just that he would have made an inference from what he saw of the general pattern; for making an inference might not get him to *see* the lines in the right way, whatever it would enable him to know about them. The learning process would have to involve a definite process of construction in which seeing has a role all along. In the same way, learning to see that an ambiguous figure had another aspect apart from the one that was initially apparent would involve a process of construction in perception, no doubt aided by the imagination, through which the second aspect is seen as related to the initial one within the total pattern. This will not give a decision procedure between learning and coming to see which will work in all cases; it gives only the general direction in which to look in seeking to arrive at a decision. It is possible, however, to generalise this account to take in ways of learning to experience things in general, and not merely seeing. To learn to experience things in ways that we have not hitherto done involves coming so to experience them but via a process of construction in which the new way of experiencing them is developed, extended, or the like, from old ways of experiencing them.

Similar things can in a way be said of learning to *do* things. New skills are built on old skills or on things that can be incorporated into skills. I make the latter qualification not to stress a difference between the acquisition of new skills and learning to experience things in new ways, but in fact to maintain a parallel. In the case of experience the old ways of experiencing things which may be used to construct the new ways of doing so need not themselves have been learned; we may just have come to experience things in those ways (the point is like the one that I made in chapter 7 about the beginnings of learning about the world, that not all coming to know need be learning). Similarly in the case of skills, what the learning may build on need not be skills previously learned; it may build on what we can do naturally. More particularly, it may build on things that we actually do or are disposed to do naturally. We can in this case treat the notion of what is natural in an entirely relative way, meaning what is natural in relation to the state of affairs existing before the skill is acquired. It is natural, for example, for adult human beings to have a number of well-established habits, which may be incorporated into a skilled performance when the latter is acquired and developed. Learning how to do something is thus the acquisition through experience of a technique in which the acquired performance is in some way a development in experience of previous performances. In this way also, what was not previously a performance in the proper sense, but, say, a passive reaction, may be taken up and made part of the performance. Thus, something that has the character of a reflex may be adapted to fit in with a more general and complex performance—when of course in the context of the wider whole it ceases to be a reflex (something that need not be surprising, since the notion of a reflex rests upon that of a reflex-arc which is an abstraction in the sense that it is treated as an isolated system artificially detached from the nervous system of which it is really a part).

I have in this reviewed in a brief and general way forms of learning other than those involved in more strictly intellectual development. In all learning, however, there is a kind of interplay between experience and understanding, a fact which I have made much of. In skills there must be some understanding of what one is engaged in, and the acquisition of the skill depends upon an interplay between that understanding and the experience that is presupposed in action at least in the form of a kind of feed-back from the action. Similar things can be said of the acquisition of new ways of experiencing things, since the new experiences could not be constructed out of the old ones without some understanding of what the experiences are of. Thus there is in a sense a growth of understanding in all learning, whether we put the emphasis on that or on the new experiences or new performances. It is difficult to think, however, that there are any rules which govern the growth of that understanding except the ones imposed by logic. I mean by this such things as the impossibility of understanding X unless Y is understood, where X logically presupposes Y. Yet even here it would be wrong to take a hard all-or-none attitude towards what understanding must involve. It may be true that where X logically presupposes Y (as, e.g., where being square logically presupposes being extended) a full understanding of X presupposes an understanding of Y, and indeed of the relationship between X and Y. It does not follow from this, however, that no understanding of X is possible where these conditions are not altogether satisfied. It is this too which reinforces the point that I have often made, that there is no sure inference from logical relationships to order of learning. Logical relationships have no necessary implications for temporal relationships, except that if understanding of X entails or presupposes understanding of Y one cannot have a full understanding of X *before* some understanding of Y; whether the understanding of Y must come before that of X is another matter. In any case, however, the possibility of degrees of understanding prevents there being any necessary temporal ordering of understanding. Does the child who understands something about the persistence of physical objects understand physics? Not much perhaps; but nothing?

The fact that there are no rules that can be established in this area means that nothing can be established *a priori* about learning beyond what is involved in understanding its very possibility. The philosophical problems in this area are problems about that possibility, not about the course of development. When we have understood the general nature of the interplay between experience and understanding that makes learning and the growth of understanding possible, there is nothing else that a philosopher can, *qua* philosopher, contribute. What is left is generalities about individuals or perhaps classes of individuals in relation to the circumstances, physical, social and cultural, that they find themselves in; and that is a matter for empirical inquiry.

One last thing before I end this chapter. Just as one can learn bad habits (although it sounds more natural to my ear to speak of picking them up), so one can learn falsehoods and false doctrines, even wrong ways of doing things.[5] The growth of understanding is not a steady progression towards sweetness and light. There are many blind alleys and incorrigible errors into which we may fall. Moreover, it may sometimes be the case that getting into a wrong position is the best way of getting out of it in such a way as to ensure that we do not fall into the trap again, or the best way of making a leap forward where otherwise there might have been a crawl. I have not laid much emphasis on such points in my discussion, but they are valid and important all the same.

10   Teaching and learning

I have so far discussed things very much from the point of view of the learner. Teaching in any explicit form has not really entered into the picture. I emphasised in connection with early learning and the beginnings of understanding how important a role must be given to adults, and I equally stressed the importance of personal relations between the child and others in this respect. It would not really be right, however, to look on what adults do in relation to babies as a form of teaching—at least, not in general. Parents and other adults do of course perform certain teaching roles in this connection: in, for example, helping the child to learn to walk, and perhaps in helping the child to learn to talk. Even in these cases, however, it may be best to put the matter as I have done, in terms of helping the child to learn, rather than teaching. Moreover, in most areas of the child's early life, what adults do and the kinds of relation that they have with him or her may help the child to learn without the adults' intentionally setting out with this aim in mind. In other words, adults may not be teaching the young children with whom they have to do, however much what they do helps them to learn.

In later learning, on the other hand, relations with adults become in general of decreasing importance for the possibility of learning, while in many areas positive teaching may become crucial if this end is to be achieved. I mean by this that, as a child grows older and acquires more knowledge and experience, so the possibilities increase of his developing and applying further what he has already acquired, although it would be wrong to think that there could be any linear relationship between such increased possibilities and age. On the other hand, the very complexities and scope of what has to be learnt may in many areas put a premium on teaching, if only for the reason that people need to be directed towards the right things and given the right kind of stimulus at the right time. Here too it is clear that personal relations may come to the fore again, but in a very different way from that in which they were requisite for early learning. Personal relations are not now a condition of learning at all, but perhaps of getting the best out of a teacher or even of getting anything that deserves the name of teaching.

It is not entirely clear, however, that they are even that. Whether or not a certain sort of relationship between teacher and taught will facilitate the teaching and learning will depend on many other conditions. It is easy to assume that teaching will proceed better where the relationship is good rather than bad, or definite rather than non-existent. Yet it is not clear that this must be so. Certain sorts of relationship may get in the way of the teaching process, and that is not true of bad relationships only. It will all depend on the individuals concerned, on what is being taught, and where the learner stands in relation to what is being taught before the teaching actually begins. This conclusion is in line with what I said in the last chapter about the impossibility of laying down anything *a priori* about how learning must proceed if it is to be successful. If that is true, teaching is necessarily an art and may well depend on *ad hoc* insights on the part of the teacher. The insights that are appropriate are likely to be quite different for different interpersonal relationships as well as for different subjects taught and for learners beginning at different points and with different initial understandings.[1]

Even if teaching is an art, however, it is not necessarily one the facility for which comes to people by nature; it may be that it can be, perhaps must be, acquired through learning. (To suppose otherwise would be to cast doubt upon the whole programme of teacher training; and although there are many with a certain scepticism about that programme, it would be foolish to think that one who has a fair knowledge of a subject needs nothing else to become a good teacher of it.) What, then, are the principles of the art which the teacher must learn or come to appreciate? There are various considerations here of different kinds depending on different aspects of what teaching is. I do not represent my distinctions as comprehensive or exhaustive, but it does seem that there are at least the following considerations. There are, first, questions arising from issues about the aims which the teacher has or must have. There are, second, questions about the content of what is or should be taught, questions which are sometimes characterised as questions about the curriculum, and these questions are not always easy to separate from those about aims. There are, third, questions about technique. Finally, there are questions about the best conditions for the successful use of technique in relation to given decisions about the curriculum and about the aims of the whole exercise. It has to be added, however, that there are also questions to be asked about how the answers to the former questions are to be fitted together, and indeed whether they can be so fitted together.

It may seem obvious what the aim of the teacher should be. What else could it be than to teach whoever it is that is being taught? It is equally clear, however, that this could at best hold only of the teacher *qua* teacher; there are many other things that those who are professional teachers have to do. Moreover, there are many other things that a teacher has to do simply *qua* teacher. He has, for example, to keep his class in order, amused, interested, happy, and with a certain concentration on the business of learning. It might be objected that these are merely subsidiary aims at best, and that their achievement is simply a means to the supreme aim of teaching people things. After all, keeping a class interested or amused would be to little point, if they did not learn anything thereby; or at all events it would be to little point if it went on like that all the time. Someone who proceeded in that way could not be said to be properly fulfilling his function as a teacher. It seems necessary that the subsidiary aims, if that is what they are, should be organised in some way.

Paul Hirst has defined 'teaching' for its central use as 'the label for those activities of a person A, the intention of which is to bring about in another person B, the intentional learning of X'.[2] This is an account of the central use, since there may be peripheral uses where one or other of the intentions referred to in the definition is missing. Hirst thinks also that the definition is subject to two further conditions; that the activities in question must be 'indicative' of X, and that it must be possible by this means for the pupil B to learn X. In other words, there must be some kind of internal relation between the activity and what is learnt, the activity must be properly describable in some way in terms of what is learnt; and learning on its basis must be possible for the pupils concerned. Unfortunately, however, it seems clear, on the other hand, that what is possible is indicated only by the success of the teaching; while, on the other hand, it is *not* clear that saying that the activity must be indicative of X or, to use my words, internally related to X says in this context any more than that it must be a teaching activity; it must be an activity from which someone could learn something of X, and not incidentally. Hence it might be said that Hirst's account comes down to the thesis that teaching is an activity that brings about learning in a teaching way, a definition that is obviously unsatisfactory because circular. We are here in a difficulty about definitions or analyses of terms that one frequently runs into in philosophy; there is a similar, well known, problem about trying to define knowledge in terms of true belief plus some other condition.[3] It is, I suggest, less an objection to the results of the procedure than to the procedure itself, that of seeking something that is a definitive analysis of the concept. What Hirst seems to be looking for is a set of necessary and sufficient conditions for an activity's constituting teaching, and it is not clear that there is such a thing. The concept of teaching is not that sort of concept.

It is, however, clear that teaching and learning are complementaries; not that the possibility of learning necessarily implies that someone is teaching, but at any rate that teaching implies that someone is learning or at least there to learn. It would not follow from this that, whatever form learning might take, there would be for this a corresponding form of teaching; it might be that for some things a person could only learn by himself, without there being the possibility of someone teaching him. At the same time, it might be held that with the qualification noted—that we are confining ourselves to those forms of learning where there is at least the possibility of teaching—there will be as many forms of teaching as there are forms of learning. What the teacher does will be efficacious as teaching to the extent that it promotes learning, and promotes it in a sense that involves more than merely making it possible.

One might invoke here an idea parallel to one that J. L. Mackie has used in connection with causality.[4] Mackie defines a cause as an insufficient but necessary part of a set of conditions which are together as a set unnecessary but sufficient for what is called the effect to follow. It may be possible to criticise some details of this as a general account of causality, and it has been so criticised by Donald Davidson[5]; but it clearly reflects some aspects of our ordinary concept of cause. If, for example, we say that the cause of a fire is someone's dropping a lighted match, it is evident that this event will be insufficient by itself to start a fire, since there has to be something to burn and sufficient oxygen to maintain a fire, as well as perhaps other things. Something of that kind, however, together with the other conditions, will be jointly sufficient for the starting of a fire, although not necessary, since a fire could be started in other ways. In a similar way, an activity performed by a person will be teaching activity provided that, while it is by itself insufficient to bring about learning, it forms a necessary part of a set of activities that together are sufficient to bring about learning, even if the learning might have been produced in other ways. The parallel is not arbitrary; for the words 'bring about' in Hirst's formulation (which is to this extent surely correct) reflect a causal notion. Hirst wished in his account to eliminate such things as opening a window as teaching activities; but the present account includes them provided that they form part of a wider activity of a kind designed to promote learning, and it seems to me that is how it should be. It is impossible to lay down in advance which activities should be counted as part of teaching and which should not; to do so might prevent genuine innovations in this area.

It seems, therefore, that all that can be said in general about the aim of the teacher, at least *qua* teacher, is that it should be to promote learning. This in itself has no necessary implications for method, or for the superiority of one method over another, unless such methods are utterly inappropriate to the promotion of learning. What, however, about the next issue, that of content? It should be clear that what I have said about aims can have no implications for this either. If, on the other hand, what can be learnt can be divided into separate and discrete areas, then this exercise *ipso facto* answers certain questions about content, although it will obviously leave unanswered questions about the importance of some areas of learning *vis-à-vis* others, and what the principles of selection between them are. Whatever be the reasons, however, why people should be taught, say, history, rather than other subjects or alongside some subjects rather than others, the determination of something as belonging to history *ipso facto* determines the sort of questions that are to be asked and in what ways the answers to them are to be sought. I do not mean to suggest that what the questions should be or are is always obvious. The practitioner of the subjects has to acquire a sort of instinct for what is the appropriate question and what is an appropriate way of answering it; that is all part of the skill that has to be acquired in becoming, say, an historian. The principles of the skill need not be explicit to the practitioner, and it may even be beneficial for the performance of the skill for them to be made explicit. (Compare what I have said in chapter 3 about knowledge of the principles involved in turning a corner on a bicycle.) The explicit formulation of the principles involved in the performance of the skill appropriate to the practice of a given discipline or subject-matter is one of the things that is the province of the philosopher of that subject. A philosopher concerned with the subject and its principles clearly has to know something, if not much, of the subject in question, but he also has to be able to abstract himself from the practice of the subject; hence, just as too much involvement in the philosophy of a subject may inhibit the practice of the subject, so may too much involvement in the practice of a subject inhibit an adequate performance of the philosopher's task.

Just as certain knowledge of a subject is a necessary condition of the pursuit of the philosophy of that subject, so a knowledge of it is necessary for a determination of how it should be taught, and what should be taught when, and for similar reasons. The successful teaching of a subject presupposes a knowledge of the questions that are appropriate to the subject and how in general one is to set about answering them. Indeed it might be said that the most important thing for the teacher is to get the pupil to think in an appropriate way: to think as an historian, a philosopher, a physicist, etc. It is not always easy to know what to do to bring this about. Philosophers know this particularly well, since because of the abstractness of the subject as well as other factors it is not at all easy to say what a philosophical question is like, and even more difficult to bring home to the uninitiated what counts as one. Some indeed would say that it is a mistake to try to delimit matters in this way: perhaps that divisions between subject-matters are to a large extent arbitrary and are often determined by extrinsic factors, such as who pays, teaching space, tradition, and so on. I do not think, however, that all such divisions are arbitrary. There are distinctions between the kinds of concept involved, between methodologies, and so on, even if it would be scholasticism to try to produce any rigid classification of forms of knowledge.[6] In fact progress sometimes depends on settling what are in effect demarcation disputes, on settling what questions are being asked or might appropriately be asked. Thus in philosophy, for example, it is sometimes important, and not just a sign of parochialism, to decide whether a given question is a philosophical one and not, say, a psychological one.

There are two objections, however, that might be made to all this. The first is that to concentrate on divisions between subjects is to beg the question against the possibility of genuine affinities between subjects. The investigation of those affinities, it may be said, might lead to a breakdown of the barriers between some, if not all, subjects; traditional distinctions should not be taken for granted. The second objection is a more radical one to the effect that thinking in this way, in terms of subjects, is wrong, and that the content of what is taught should be decided on other grounds.

It is important to be clear on what the issues are here. If one is concerned simply with the question of what can be taught, then a division into different subjects gives one sort of answer, along the lines of 'Many different things, but the possibilities are as follows, and the differences arise for the following reasons'. Even so, such an answer would be in a sense restrictive, since many things that can be taught—tricks, knacks, skills, trades, appreciation, taste (to mention but some)—do not always or characteristically admit of classification on the basis of subjects. To think in terms of subjects is to think in academic terms, that is to say in terms dictated by the conception of a public body of knowledge, presumably advancing with the progress of research. It is a conception in which the divisions and interrelationships are determined from above, by what happens in universities and research institutes, in terms of what is seen to be the case at the frontiers of knowledge. There is combined with this the idea that the subject should bring with it a body of theory. It is for this reason that some look with suspicion at those subjects of which this is less true than they think it should be, and where, for example, a good deal of time is devoted to practical skills, e.g. languages. From this point of view, those who object to the division into subjects may do so either because they think that the advance of knowledge is hindered by compartmentalisation or because they think it educationally vicious. The more radical objection that I noted above is more naturally connected with the educational issues, while the more moderate objection could be connected with either the educational or the research issues. It is scarcely conceivable, however, that one concerned with the advance of knowledge should advocate the breakdown of all divisions of the subject-matter of knowledge.

As one gets further away from a simple concern for the advance of knowledge, however, the more there are likely to be pressures against compartmentalisation for varying reasons. Views on what one should teach children may be influenced, if not determined, by a variety of factors. There is, for example, the consideration that the children may come to be participants in the advance of knowledge of which I have spoken, or some of them at least; and for this reason it may well seem desirable that it should at least be made possible for them to do so. There is, however, the counter-consideration that many, if not most of them, will not be in a position to do so. On the other hand, there are a number of skills and abilities that are useful in a variety of ways in life, and other abilities that may, as is generally thought to be the case of artistic appreciation if not artistic performance, lead to the enhancement of life. There is, finally, a consideration adduced by some, that the aim of the exercise is not anything of this sort but rather the flowering of the individual, the actualisation of whatever potentialities he has, his becoming a good member of society, a good sharer in personal relations, or what have you. Different ideals are likely to produce different conceptions of what education is for and what it is about. I do not intend here to make any comment on these different ideals. It is clear, however, that any educational policy is likely in practice to be a compromise.

It will be a compromise if only because ideals are likely to be up against the limitations imposed by such considerations as (to mention some selected almost at random) the differences between pupils, the availability of able and willing teachers, the availability of suitable periods of time and sufficient material and space. Hence it is inevitably necessary to determine priorities, and it is less than clear how these are to be established on the basis of ideals alone. At the academic level, an expert in a given area or subject may be in the position, given sufficient thought on the matter, to reach a conclusion about what the priorities are as regards learning, if someone is to become moderately competent, or even expert, within that area or subject. He may, however, be faced with demands, and these days often is so faced, from various quarters for a justification of the claim that the units in terms of which priorities are to be assessed are to be construed as they are by him. Criticisms of certain academic subjects on the grounds of their lack of 'relevance' are in effect criticisms of this kind. If something is relevant, it is relevant *to* something, and the criticism of a subject or part of a subject that it lacks relevance is a criticism to the effect that it has low priority in relation to some wider unit. On the other hand, the suggestion that students should be free to choose the way in which they build up their studies presupposes, if it is to have any meaning, a range of offerings from which choice can be made. This in turn raises the question whether and to what extent units of choice can genuinely be available, without any prior decision having been made about priorities. Unfortunately, here too, other factors are likely to determine what is to count as a unit, factors such as the amount of time available, and perhaps, though not necessarily, the problems of assessment. It would be a mistake to suppose that decisions on matters of this kind that are appropriate for one area of knowledge are necessarily equally valid for others.

In sum, except where what is to be taught and how it is to be taught are determined by a conception of a relatively autonomous and independent subject-matter, it is difficult to see how any firm principles of curriculum planning can be established. Any decisions on curricula are likely in these circumstances to have to be made on the basis of a variety of considerations; and this likelihood ought to be faced. It is not clear in particular that one can correlate different disciplines with the development of distinct mental powers, whether or not it is possible at all to distinguish mental powers in this way.[7] If it is at least one of the functions of the teacher to encourage the development of such mental powers, it is not obvious that the goal can be achieved by curriculum planning rather than good teaching. Moreover, attempts at *a priori* integration of curriculum on this basis may do more harm than good. At an advanced level, interdisciplinary studies often turn out to be exceptionally difficult for the student, and where profitable integration occurs it sometimes, if not always, occurs in ways that were not initially expected. At a less advanced level, attempts at integration may lead to fragmentation instead; for the student may not know enough of anything to make connections profitably. To say this is not to attempt to put an embargo on such projects; it is to say that they should at least be treated experimentally, since there is no way of arriving at sound decisions *a priori*. That is indeed what philosophical considerations would suggest; for anything that can be decided *a priori* must rest on *conceptual* connections. Given a definite conception of a goal and an understanding of what that goal presupposes in consequence it is possible to reach *a priori* a conclusion about what will have to be done for a full attainment of that goal. Nevertheless, as I have tried to make clear often in the foregoing, it does not follow from this that any conclusions can be reached about the order in which the necessary steps must be taken or to the effect that taking these steps in some order will necessarily be the way or the only way of reaching the goal. One cannot limit *a priori* the ways in which understanding can be attained. It is perhaps wise in such circumstances to keep an open mind about curricula and as far as possible keep one's options open. There may still be areas in which the range of options is more circumscribed than in others—and understandably so in view of the nature of the subject in question—but some options nevertheless remain.

It may be thought that in the last few pages I have got away from what I should, strictly speaking, be concerned with. Was not my real concern with the content of teaching *per se*, and have I not become concerned with wider issues in the philosophy of education? In a way this is true. In the abstract all that one can say about the content of teaching is that one can teach whatever can be learnt (in principle, if not in practice); and one can learn (again in principle) whatever can be known through, in some way, experience (where experience includes the effects of teaching). What can be known differs according to whether it is theoretical or practical, according to the different concepts involved and the different rationalia for truth, and so on. Each of these differences has some implications for learning, and therefore for teaching. It would be foolish to think that one could teach a practical skill like typing or playing a musical instrument in the same way that one teaches mathematiçs or theoretical physics. All this is true, although in each case there has to be some kind of blend of knowledge of general principles, knowledge of techniques and knowledge of how these are applied to cases, with differing emphases on one or other of these for different forms of knowledge.[8] While, however, from the point of view of the content of teaching in the abstract it would perhaps be sufficient simply to point to the differences between forms of knowledge and thus to differences in what can be taught, someone concerned with the growth of understanding might justifiably be called upon to have some concern for the relations between forms of knowledge and the implications of these for general educational practice. This remains true even if my conclusions about it all are in a sense pessimistic.

If the sort of thing that Piaget says about the stages is anything like true, it would surely be a simple mistake to attempt to teach certain things at certain stages of a child's life. I do not mean by this merely that it would be a mistake to try to teach theoretical physics to a child of four, but that it would be a mistake to try to teach anything abstract to a child of that age. I noted in chapter 4 Bruner's claim that it is possible to teach anything to a child of any age provided that one sets about it in the right way. The objection to trying to teach a four-year-old child theoretical physics is that he could not possibly know enough about the physical world or about the apparatus necessary for understanding it at that age; but it surely would not be true that he does not know *anything* about it. The problem is to discover what he does know and build on that, with the knowledge that it may be a very long process. Similar considerations apply to the point that the child could not understand anything abstract. He could not think abstractly enough—but not at all? Perhaps not enough to notice, but it remains true that the power of thinking abstractly is not something that emerges fully developed only after other stages have been passed through. Once again one has to discover what is there and build on that. That is why some teachers can do so much more than others—or one reason at least. It requires immense percipience, sensitivity, tact, and of course patience.

In his article 'What is teaching?'[9] Hirst gives as an example of what would *not* be teaching; the instance of reading to a class of six-year-olds sections from Wittgenstein's *Philosophical Investigations* in order to teach Wittgenstein's criticisms of the idea of a private language. The class, he says, would just not be in the position to learn anything on the matter. One's immediate reaction is likely to be 'Of course, not with normal six-year-olds anyway'. The qualification, however, is important. In some circumstances to try to teach certain things would just be daft, but it would be a great mistake to let this general consideration inhibit one from trying things that may at first sight look impossible. In some circumstances there is virtue in trying to teach people things that they cannot understand; perhaps something will get home and in a way that might not have been anticipated. Human understanding and its development being what they are, it is a mistake always to make things easy and perhaps a mistake always to make them clear. That should not be taken as an excuse for slovenly obscurity. It is just that one cannot always be sure where the rewards may come, and a stimulus to thought may work in surprising ways. The art of the teacher is to have a nice estimate of the situation in the right circumstances.

Thus the sort of answer that is relevant to the question 'What should one teach people as part of their education?' becomes relevant also to the question 'What should one teach people as part of instruction in subject X?' The answer is, 'Well, it depends on many factors, some of which will lie outside your control and may turn on practical and other considerations which may seem irrelevant. While, however, you may be able to formulate for yourself some general principles, do not inhibit yourself from being experimental, and keep your options open as far as you can.' Once again it is doubtful whether there is much, if anything, that can be established and laid down *a priori*.

In a certain sense I have, in what I have just been saying, also had things to say about the third class of issues about teaching that I noted at the beginning: issues about technique. In many respects questions concerning content and questions concerning technique of teaching are inseparable. That is why it is the case that where the content of a subject becomes involved, complex and technical in a way that requires an expertise if it is to be grasped, there is little that an outsider can offer concerning teaching technique. I do not mean to suggest by this that there is *nothing* that can be offered. There is practical experience in the area; there are little but important things such as being audible, interesting and as far as possible intelligible; there are things such as being able to use a blackboard or other visual aids and knowing when they are relevant; and there are things such as having a correct judgment about the relative amount of time to be given to exposition and comment in relation to a particular audience. Not all these things can be taught in any formal way, although a stimulus may be given to the teacher to think about the issues. It is, however, common consent, I believe, that the most important part of the training of a teacher is guided practice; and this is what might be expected, if, as I have been insisting, teaching is an art. A teacher needs certain natural talents and a certain personality without which nobody could become a teacher; for the rest he needs mainly, though not entirely, to be put in the position of making good use of what he has.

As I have said before, it is clear that knowing a subject backwards is not a sufficient condition of being able to teach it, although it is sometimes (though not by any means always) true that there is more to be got from what may seem more or less the ramblings of a genius than from the well-organised remarks of a more pedestrian mind. That, however, depends on, among other things, the ability of the learners to recognise and pick up gems when they see them, and sometimes the gems are too covered with mud for anyone to see them for what they are. Yet while knowledge of a subject is not in general a sufficient condition of being able to teach it, a certain knowledge of it seems to be a necessary condition of being able to teach it. How much knowledge however?

As Gilbert Ryle has emphasised in his admirable article on 'Teaching and Training'[10], it is the supreme reward of the teacher 'to turn out from time to time the student who comes to be not merely abreast of his teacher but ahead of him'. Ryle has in mind a student at the higher levels of learning, but in a certain sense the same applies at other levels too; for teaching is not just imparting what the teacher knows or has to offer, it is also getting the student to go beyond. Hence the best result of teaching is the imparting of that kind of understanding which is taken up and used to achieve further results that have not been directly brought about by the teacher. If this can be achieved on whatever basis it does not really matter whether the teacher himself knows what he has thus indirectly brought about. The experience which every teacher, at least at certain levels and over a certain time span, must have had, when the pupil sees just that bit further than the teacher himself has done, can be a humiliating one, but on reflection a rewarding one too. It is indeed the real aim of the exercise. Its possibility distinguishes teaching from mere training, as Ryle was anxious to emphasise. It equally distinguishes the teacher from the guru; for, while a teacher has pupils, a guru has disciples, and whereas disciples, by definition, retain a kind of dependence on and relation to their master, this need not be so, and perhaps should not be so, of pupils.

That is not to say that a teacher has not got information or even doctrine to hand on. Handing on doctrine, however, need not be indoctrination; not even the handing on of doctrine with the intention that pupils should accept it. It depends very much on the spirit with which it is done. There are lots of things that teachers have to do as necessary conditions of other things. It may be necessary, for example, for pupils to be got to learn things by rote, or in certain practical activities to learn things by rote in a fairly automatic way. Equally it may be necessary for pupils to be got to accept certain things as a condition of going on to other things. That does not matter at all provided that the opportunity exists of coming back to review the initial beliefs or activities in a larger context. Of course it is not always practicable that one should do this in an effective way; some early beliefs and ways of behaving become so well embedded that it is extremely difficult, if not impossible, to modify them, let alone shake them off. This is a fact that teachers should at least be aware of, and they should be prepared to modify practice accordingly if necessary. It is not, however, a reason for abstaining from inculcating beliefs altogether or from handing on information altogether; it is not a reason for having nothing to do with rote learning or, at certain points, drill. It *is* a reason for not making these things anything approaching the whole of learning. At certain points, at all levels, questioning and criticism have to be encouraged, provided, of course, that the questioning and criticism are initiated in the spirit of serious inquiry. Accusations made in certain quarters, however, that teachers must necessarily in the nature of the case indoctrinate their pupils are just silly.

To the extent that the aim of teaching is to inculcate in pupils and students both knowledge and understanding of the subject-matter under consideration or the mastery of a technique which is more than doing something by rote, the teacher must have a certain responsiveness to the needs of those who are learning, if his teaching is to be effective. Yet this is necessarily a matter of judgment. Child-centred teaching and child-centred education, which have become the focus of a whole educational movement, are practices which put all the weight on the needs of the child— and not always the child construed simply as a learner. Yet even apart from the facts that the needs of the child are not always all that obvious, and that there are the demands inherent in the body of public knowledge and the techniques that are put before the child as part of education, there is, as I have emphasised before, some reason for not looking *all the time* at what the child is able to take. That a responsiveness to the learner is for a good deal of the time *de rigueur* needs hardly saying, but what has to be taught brings its own demands apart from those coming from the child.

That is even more true at the level of higher education. That is not to say that a student-centred higher education makes no sense at all; but the higher one goes in education the more the demands of the subject become pressing. The idea, for example, that the degree of doctor of philosophy or doctor of science should be tailored to the student would make no sense at all. What institutions of higher education have as their main function is something that can be argued about, but higher learning is not the same as higher education; and if universities do not have as one of their main functions the pursuit of higher learning—the pursuit of knowledge for its own sake and the participation in this by students at all levels to some extent or other—it is difficult to know what universities are about. If this is elitism, so be it; but why it should involve elitism in any vicious sense it is hard to see. University teaching, like any other teaching, is likely to be a compromise between responses to different demands from different sources, but if an institution forgets altogether the demands inherent in the pursuit of knowledge it no longer deserves the name of 'university'.

It should be clear from all this that the techniques of teaching must inevitably vary according to the subject, the level at which it is being taught, the sort of people it is being taught to, and the circumstances in which the teaching takes place. There is no such thing as a single model for teaching or a single concept of teaching, apart from the general aim that the teacher must have as a teacher. Except for this consideration, what teaching is must inevitably vary according to the factors that I have mentioned. Hence my discussion of the third issue concerning teaching (technique) has strayed over into the area of the fourth (the conditions for success), just as happened with the other issues. There is little to be added on the fourth issue, for the moral is the same: the conditions for success are very various and cannot profitably be discussed except in the context of the other issues. If my conclusions seem unduly pacificatory in relation to different attitudes to the subject and too unwilling to come to a definite answer to each question, I can reply only by saying that that is how the situation appears to me when approached in this general way. There might be more illumination to be gained by confining one's attention to specific areas of teaching under specific conditions. To do that, however, is not my present concern, which is with the general place of teaching in the context of the growth of understanding.

Let me try to sum up my discussion in relation to that aim. As I

143

said at the beginning of this chapter, teaching must play a larger and larger part as what has to be known and understood becomes more technical and more abstruse. It is also required on occasion in order to open up a whole new way of proceeding through a single technique. Perhaps the most obvious instance of this is reading. Some children more or less teach themselves to read as long as they are put in the way of doing so. Reading, however, is, amongst other things, a skill that depends upon a recognition and acceptance of publicly agreed rules and conventions. Hence if a child picks it up without explicit teaching he has to be in the position to appreciate and go by those rules and conventions; and he has somehow to be put in the way of this even if he is not explicitly taught. However the child comes by the ability to read, once he has acquired the technique a whole new area of knowledge and understanding is opened up that would not otherwise be available. There are clearly other instances of this sort of thing, instances of techniques and forms of understanding that make possible sudden progressions forward on a wide front. The growth of understanding is not a gradual and steadily progressive business. One can point to crucial factors and stages in it, but there are no rules as to how it should proceed throughout. So much depends upon teaching at certain times and in relation to certain factors in the understanding.

The fact that it plays a part at all, however, is one reason why it is implausible to think of the growth of understanding in terms of any simple relationship between genesis and structure or in terms of these ideas alone. Much will depend for a child on what teaching it receives, and this is a kind of contingent fact affecting its experience that makes implausible the idea of a structured genesis *simpliciter*. On the other hand, it is not right to count this sort of factor as just one among the contingencies of experience, how experience happens to fall. Teaching is one of the immense social influences that affect a child, but its effects can be out of proportion to any other kind of social influence once the first beginnings of a child's life are past. In it once again knowledge builds on knowledge, but the form of experience that makes it possible is really quite unlike those forms of experience that come the individual's way when teaching is not involved. There is the experience that simply comes to an individual; there is that which he is put in the way of, as a child is by way of the relations that he has with adults and other children; and there is teaching. The feat that the young child performs in learning to talk without much, if anything, of positive teaching is an immense one, but it is incommensurate with later feats that are performed as a result of teaching. It is hard to overestimate the importance of teaching in an individual human being's upbringing.

11 Conclusion

I have said nothing in the foregoing about all sorts of dimensions of human life in which the growth of understanding plays a part. I have said nothing, for example, of the growth of moral or social understanding. I have said little, apart from what I have said about what holds good at the beginning of life, about the part played by emotional factors and what emotional development is to be seen as, if anything. The reason is that these matters open up large areas of their own. It would scarcely make sense to try to say something about the growth of moral understanding without a clear view about what morality consists in; whether, for example, it consists in conformity to moral rules and principles, whatever be their nature, or whether it involves a more complex view of human life and some picture of what a human being is. Piaget has had things to say about moral development so-called, as well as about other developmental issues. (I say 'so-called' because it may be that here doubts about the use of the term 'development' reach their height. For further remarks on this see my paper 'The Concept of Development' referred to in chapter 1 above.) He views it as a development of the individual through the idea of doing things because adults say so, then the idea of doing things because there is a rule to that effect, and finally to the idea of the tempering of the rule with justice and equity. Refinements have been added to this scheme by Kohlberg.[1] It cannot be denied, however, that this picture presupposes a view about what the progression is a progression towards, as well indeed as the view that it is in fact a progression; and many would hold that this view leaves much to be desired, or at any rate is an over-simple view of human life and moral considerations. A view of the growth of moral understanding necessarily involves and presupposes a view about morality, and it would therefore be rash to enter the field without a developed moral philosophy. The same applies to the other areas that I have mentioned.

For that reason I have judged it best to confine myself to the more explicitly epistemological issues. It might plausibly be held that a philosophical question typically has the form 'How is X possible?'. For this reason it seemed to me that the crucial philosophical concern in this area is with the question 'How is learning and the growth of understanding through experience possible?' Consequently I have concentrated on the problem of how learning gets started at all; for this is the prime philosophical problem in this area. The subsequent pattern of 'No learning without prior knowledge', and of knowledge being built on knowledge itself provokes the question of how it can ever get started. The problem that was stated in Plato's *Meno* is therefore central, and classical epistemological theories suggest possible solutions to it in their terms. Contemporary responses to classical epistemologies, particularly perhaps those stimulated by Wittgenstein, equally suggest possible comments on the solutions to the problem of learning put forward in terms of those classical epistemologies. It might justly be said that this is what my discussion comes to.

Let me say again that I have not intended to trespass on ground covered by and perhaps reserved for psychologists and other empirical investigators. There are many questions in this area that can be answered only after much empirical inquiry and a just respect for the empirical facts. Nevertheless, the question 'How is learning possible?' and questions of the same kind are proper philosophical questions; and it might even be hoped that the answers to them will provide a framework which empirical investigators might conceivably find useful.

One final point: I have said little, except perhaps implicitly, about many of the things that are dealt with by psychologists under the heading of learning. Except in chapter 2 I have said little overtly, for example, about conditioning, although many would classify this as a learning process. This is because I see a connection between learning and understanding or knowledge; even learning to do something seems to involve acquiring some understanding or knowledge of the principles of the activity. This *ex hypothesi* rules out conditioning as having anything to do with learning.[2] I do not think that this is mere legislation on my part, and I have tried to indicate in chapter 9 how the point about knowledge can be taken care of when we are concerned with learning to have appreciation of things, to have certain attitudes to things, or to see things in certain ways. Moreover, I would not deny that natural or habitual reactions can be made use of in learned activities. At the same time, it seems to me that to say that someone has learnt to withdraw his hand from an object on hearing a sound, when that sound has initially been associated with an incipient electric shock, is to say more than that he has been conditioned to do so. Or at all events this is so with the classical theory of conditioning, while extended accounts of conditioning such as that involved in the operant conditioning espoused by Skinner do not have enough in common with classical conditioning for the word 'conditioning' to be more than a homonym in consequence. It cannot be denied that Skinner has originated many teaching devices built on his notion of an operant or chains of operants; what this shows about the theory that lies behind them is another matter, and what it shows about his general philosophy of man is another matter again. I make no apology for confining my discussion of his ideas to what I have said in chapter 2.

Some might say, nevertheless, that my conception of learning is a sophisticated one, and that I reserve the term for fairly high-level, and certainly human, forms of learning. I do not believe that this is true. As far as animals are concerned, I believe that the story that I have given has application to them *mutatis mutandis*, and one of the *mutata* will have to do with the extent to which the notion of learning gets application to animals at all. That it does get application to many animals is clear, but not all modifications of animal behaviour are properly construable as the result of learning. Once again, however, the details of this issue lie outside my main concern. If the term 'learning' were to cause difficulty I should be happy to drop it. The main question, to the answer to which I hope that I have contributed something at least, is the philosophical question 'How is it possible that human beings should acquire knowledge and understanding as the result of experience?' How, that is, are we to understand that possibility? For it is one of the great things about human beings that it *is* possible.

Notes and references

Full publication details of works cited here will be found in the Bibliography

Introduction

1 One might invoke, however, in this connection what J. Bowlby has claimed about the effects of maternal deprivation at a crucial stage of childhood on subsequent character development. See J. Bowlby, *Child Care and the Growth of Love*.
2 Cf. D.W. Hamlyn, *Sensation and Perception*, p. 60.
3 See, e.g., L. Wittgenstein, *Philosophical Investigations*, I, 242.
4 Bertrand Russell, *Logic and Knowledge* (ed. R.C. Marsh), p. 195.
5 Cf., for example, Noam Chomsky's remark in *Language and Mind*, p. 74, where he speaks of the child having to discover language 'from the data presented to him'.

2 Genesis without structure

1 Cf. Aristotle's *De Anima*, 432a, 3ff. The suggestions are not, in my opinion, unequivocal.
2 See Aristotle, *Posterior Analytics*, II, 10 and 11. The ways in question are expounded in his doctrine of the four causes or four kinds of reason why.
3 Cf. the remark that opens the *Posterior Analytics*; 'All teaching and all intellectual learning come about from previously existing knowledge'.
4 See D.W. Hamlyn, 'Aristotelian Epagoge', *Phronesis*, vol. 21 (1976), pp. 167–84.
5 See Aristotle, *Metaphysics*, Θ , 2.
6 Cf. P. Geach, *Mental Acts*, sections 10 and 11, and D.W. Hamlyn, *The Theory of Knowledge*, esp. pp. 40–2.
7 For doubts about the whole notion, see D.W. Hamlyn, 'Conditioning and Behaviour', in R. Borger and F. Cioffi (eds), *Explanation in the Behavioural Sciences*. Skinner first developed his ideas in *The Behavior of Organisms* (1938); see also his *Verbal Behavior* (1957).
8 See G. Ryle, *The Concept of Mind*, ch. 2.

3 Structure without genesis

1 See D.W. Hamlyn, *The Psychology of Perception*, chs 3 and 4.
2 Theodore Mischel, in his remarks as chairman of the symposium on 'Human Learning' to which I contributed along with John Morton, some of whose remarks on the same matter are also relevant. See S.C. Brown (ed.), *The Philosophy of Psychology*, esp. pp. 175ff.
3 See S.P. Stich, 'What Every Speaker Knows', *Philosophical Review* (1971), pp. 476ff.
4 I say 'so-called *a priori* ideas' because I think that the whole distinction between *a priori* and *a posteriori* ideas is in fact suspect; see my *Theory of Knowledge*, p. 58.

4 Genesis with structure

1 For a contrary view, see Stephen Toulmin's contribution to T. Mischel (ed.), *Human Action*, and my criticism of it, together with Toulmin's reply, in T. Mischel (ed.), *Cognitive Development and Epistemology*.
2 For example, see J. Piaget, *The Principles of Genetic Epistemology*, pp. 47ff.
3 The idea has what is perhaps its most literal application in connection with visual perception, and is used by Piaget in that way in his *Mechanisms of Perception*.
4 J. Piaget, *Biology and Knowledge*, p. 17.
5 D.W. Hamlyn, in T. Mischel (ed.), *Cognitive Development and Epistemology*, p. 20.
6 Ibid., for T. Mischel's contribution on these notions.
7 R. Borger and A.E.M. Seabourne, *The Psychology of Learning*, p. 96.
8 Bruner himself recognises stages of intellectual development which have some kinship with Piaget's, but he does not think that they have the same kind of necessity or relationship to age. See, for example, his *Beyond the Information Given* (ed. J.M. Anglin).
9 See J. Piaget, *Biology and Knowledge*, p. 20.
10 See, for example, J. Piaget, *Structuralism*, p. 139.
11 Cf., for example, J. Piaget, *The Mechanisms of Perception*, p. 364; *The Principles of Genetic Epistemology*, p. 82; *Biology and Knowledge*, pp. 64–5.
12 See p. 10 above, and the paper on 'The Concept of Development' there cited.
13 Compare Aristotle's claim that knowledge of the particular is prior to knowledge of the general: prior in relation to us, although not necessarily prior in itself. There are, however, differences between particularity and concreteness to which I shall return in chapter 9.
14 See D.W. Hamlyn in T. Mischel (ed.), *Cognitive Development and Epistemology*, pp. 21–2.
15 Cf. Wittgenstein's notion of 'agreement in judgments', *Philosophical Investigations*, I, 242.

5 **Experience and understanding: I Perception**

1 See D.W. Hamlyn, *Sensation and Perception* for a survey of these issues.

2 T. Reid, *Essays on the Intellectual Powers of Man*, I, 1.

3 Ibid., II, 5.

4 See, on the other side, the papers by F. Sibley and J.W. Roxbee Cox in F. Sibley (ed.), *Perception*.

5 For further considerations on the place of sensations *vis-à-vis* judgment in perception, see D.W. Hamlyn, 'Unconscious Inference and Judgment in Perception', a paper given to the University of Western Ontario Workshop on 'Images, Perception and Knowledge', May 1974, reprinted in J.M. Nicholas (ed.), *Images, Perception and Knowledge*.

6 I have tried to say more about it in the paper cited in the previous note.

6 **Experience and understanding: II Concepts and their conditions**

1 See D.W. Hamlyn, *The Theory of Knowledge*, pp. 93–5.

2 'Courtesy attribution' is a phrase that I have heard used in this context, but I cannot remember by whom. Cf. *The Theory of Knowledge*, p. 207. For a treatment of the similar suggestion that what is being attributed is so in a 'logically secondary sense', see D.M. Armstrong, *Belief, Truth and Knowledge*, pp. 28ff.

3 P. Geach, *Mental Acts*, p. 17.

4 Cf. also Zeno Vendler, *Res Cogitans*, ch. 4.

5 See L.S. Vygotsky, 'Thought and Word', reprinted in Parveen Adams (ed.), *Language in Thinking*, pp. 180ff., esp. p. 186.

6 I have discussed the same point in 'Person Perception and Our Understanding of Others', in T. Mischel (ed.), *Understanding Other Persons*, pp. 32–3.

7 See, however, D.E. Cooper, 'Grammar and the Possession of Concepts', *Proceedings of the Philosophy of Education Society of Great Britain* (1973), pp. 204ff.

8 C. Taylor, *The Explanation of Behaviour*, p. 68. See also his contribution to T. Mischel (ed.), *Cognitive Development and Epistemology*, esp. pp. 404ff.

9 See the discussion of 'Washoe' in R.A. Gardner and B.T. Gardner, 'Teaching Sign Language to a Chimpanzee', *Science* (1969), reprinted in Parveen Adams (ed.), *Language in Thinking*, pp. 17ff.

10 W. Köhler, *The Mentality of Apes*.

11 Wittgenstein (*Philosophical Investigations*, II, 174) seems to express doubt about the attribution of hope to a dog, and if so I cannot see the grounds for such scepticism; he may, however, be confining the scepticism to the idea that a dog can hope for something the day after tomorrow, and in that case the difficulties lie in ascribing the concept of the day after tomorrow to a dog, not in ascribing hope to it *simpliciter*.

12 See, for example, Zeno Vendler, *Res Cogitans*, ch. 5; and A.R. White, 'What We Believe', *Studies in the Philosophy of Mind, American Philosophical Quarterly*, Monograph series No. 6 (1972). The distinction is, however, in reality an ancient and hoary one.

13 L. Wittgenstein, *Philosophical Investigations*, I, 242.

14 Wittgenstein's *On Certainty* is in many ways an elaboration of that theme.

15 For more on this theme, see D.W. Hamlyn, 'Person Perception and Our Understanding of Others', in T. Mischel (ed.), *Understanding Other Persons*.

7 The beginnings of understanding

1 See, for example, D.W. Hamlyn, *The Theory of Knowledge*, ch. 3.

2 In these remarks I owe something to a paper by a student of mine, Mr Peter Janke.

3 For such a suggestion, see John Rawls, *A Theory of Justice*, p. 463.

4 If one seeks for a classical theory of human nature which will reflect this, one might discover it in Bishop Butler's theory of particular propensities to such things as benevolence, rather than in Hobbes's hedonism. I have suggested this in my contribution to T. Mischel (ed.), *Understanding Other Persons*, p. 25.

8 Language

1 See, for example, J. Piaget, 'Language and Thought from the Genetic Point of View', *Acta Psychologica* (1954), reprinted in Parveen Adams (ed.), *Language in Thinking*, pp. 170ff.

9 Later learning

1 I was perhaps not clear on this point in my 'Logical and Psychological Aspects of Learning', in R.S. Peters (ed.), *The Concept of Education*.

2 See further on this my remarks in T. Mischel (ed.), *Cognitive Development and Epistemology*, pp. 19ff., and my paper cited in the previous note.

3 Cf., for example, some of R.S. Peters' remarks in 'Freedom and the Development of the Free Man', reprinted in his *Psychology and Ethical Development*, pp. 336ff., esp. pp. 354ff. See also his 'Moral Development and Moral Learning', *Monist*, 58 ((1974), pp. 541–67, esp. p. 542.

4 See particularly Donald Davidson, 'Actions, Reasons and Causes', *Journal of Philosophy* (1963), reprinted in A.R. White (ed.), *The Philosophy of Action*.

5 Cf. S.C. Brown, 'Learning', *PASS* (1972), pp. 19ff.

10 **Teaching and learning**

1 Since I wrote this there has appeared *Education and Personal Relationships* by R.S. Downie, Eileen M. Loudfoot and Elizabeth Telfer. The book has things to say which are relevant both to these issues and to other things discussed in this chapter.

2 P.H. Hirst, 'What is Teaching?', reprinted in R.S. Peters (ed.), *The Philosophy of Education*, p. 172. Papers by Hirst are now collected in his *Knowledge and the Curriculum*.

3 See D.W. Hamlyn, *The Theory of Knowledge*, ch. 4. A great deal of discussion of this issue in recent times has stemmed from a paper by E.L. Gettier in *Analysis* (1963), reprinted in A.P. Griffiths (ed.), *Knowledge and Belief*, pp. 144ff.

4 J.L. Mackie, 'Causes and Conditions', *American Journal of Philosophy* (1965), pp. 245ff.

5 D. Davidson, 'Causal Relations', *Journal of Philosophy* (1967), pp. 691ff.

6 Cf. P.H. Hirst, 'Liberal Education and the Nature of Knowledge', reprinted in R.S. Peters (ed.), *The Philosophy of Education*, pp. 87ff. I am far from accusing Hirst himself of scholasticism, but it is easy to see how the approach could become this.

7 Ibid., p. 95. But see also R.K. Elliott 'Education and Human Being' in S.C. Brown (ed.), *Philosophers Discuss Education*.

8 See D.W. Hamlyn, 'Logical and Psychological Aspects Learning', in R.S. Peters (ed.), *The Philosophy of Education*, pp. 195ff., especially the observations on the relation between learning a subject and understanding its underlying principles.

9 Hirst, 'What is Teaching', op. cit., p. 173.

10 G. Ryle, 'Teaching and Training', in R.S. Peters (ed.), *The Concept of Education*; cf. also M. Oakeshott's 'Learning and Teaching' in the same volume.

11 **Conclusion**

1 See, for example, the contribution by L. Kohlberg in T. Mischel (ed.), *Cognitive Development and Epistemology*.

2 See on this G.N.A. Vesey, 'Conditioning and Learning', in R.S. Peters (ed.), *The Concept of Education*, pp. 61ff., and D.W. Hamlyn, 'Conditioning and Behaviour', in R. Borger and F. Cioffi (eds.), *Explanation in the Behavioural Sciences*, pp. 139ff. The remarks about conditioning that follow are in small part a summary of the argument of the paper.

Bibliography of works cited

ADAMS, PARVEEN (ed.), *Language in Thinking*, Penguin, Harmondsworth, 1972.

ARISTOTLE, *De Anima*.

ARISTOTLE, *Nicomachean Ethics*.

ARISTOTLE, *Metaphysics*.

ARISTOTLE, *Posterior Analytics*.

ARMSTRONG, D. M., *Perception and the Physical World*, Routledge & Kegan Paul, London, 1961.

ARMSTRONG, D. M., *The Materialist Theory of Mind*, Routledge & Kegan Paul, London, 1968.

ARMSTRONG, D. M., *Belief, Truth and Knowledge*, Cambridge University Press, 1973.

AUNE, B., *Knowledge, Mind and Nature*, Random House, New York, 1967.

BORGER, R. and CIOFFI, F. (eds), *Explanation in the Behavioural Sciences*, Cambridge University Press, 1970.

BORGER, R. and SEABOURNE, A. E. M., *The Psychology of Learning*, Penguin, Harmondsworth, 1966.

BOWLBY, J., *Child Care and the Growth of Love*, Penguin, Harmondsworth, 1953.

BROWN, S. C., 'Learning', *Proceedings of the Aristotelian Society*, supp. vol. 46 (1972), pp. 19-39.

BROWN, S. C. (ed.), *The Philosophy of Psychology*, Macmillan, London and Basingstoke, 1973.

BROWN, S. C. (ed.), *Philosophers Discuss Education*, Macmillan, London and Basingstoke, 1975.

BRUNER, J., *Beyond the Information Given*, ed. J. M. Anglin, Allen & Unwin, London, 1974.

CHISHOLM, R., *Perceiving*, Cornell University Press, Ithaca, NY, 1957; Oxford University Press, London.

CHOMSKY, N., *Language and Mind*, Harcourt Brace, New York, 1968.

COOPER, D. E., 'Grammar and the Possession of Concepts', *Proceedings of the Philosophy of Education Society of Great Britain*, vol. 7 (1973), pp. 204-22.

DAVIDSON, D., 'Actions, Reasons and Causes', *Journal of Philosophy*, vol. 60 (1963), pp. 685-700.

DAVIDSON, D., 'Causal Relations', *Journal of Philosophy*, vol. 64 (1967), pp. 691-703.

DOWNIE, R. S., LOUDFOOT, EILEEN M. and TELFER, ELIZABETH, *Education and Personal Relationships*, Methuen, London, 1974.

DRETSKE, F., *Seeing and Knowing*, Routledge & Kegan Paul, London, 1969.

GEACH, P., *Mental Acts*, Routledge & Kegan Paul, London, 1957.

154

GETTIER, E. L., 'Is Justified True Belief Knowledge?', *Analysis*, vol. 23 (1963), pp. 121–3.

GREGORY, R., *Eye and Brain*, Weidenfeld & Nicolson, London, 1966.

GRIFFITHS, A. P. (ed.), *Knowledge and Belief*, Oxford University Press, London, 1967.

HAMLYN, D. W., *The Psychology of Perception*, Routledge & Kegan Paul, London, 1957.

HAMLYN, D. W., 'The Visual Field and Perception', *Proceedings of the Aristotelian Society*, supp. vol. 31 (1957), pp. 107–24.

HAMLYN, D. W., *Sensation and Perception*, Routledge & Kegan Paul, London, 1961.

HAMLYN, D. W., *The Theory of Knowledge*, Macmillan, London and Basingstoke, 1971; Doubleday, New York.

HAMLYN, D. W., 'Aristotelian Epagoge', *Phronesis*, vol. 21 (1976), pp. 167–84.

HAMLYN, D. W., 'The Concept of Development', *Proceedings of the Philosophy of Education Society of Great Britain*, vol. ix (1975), pp. 26–39.

HAMLYN, D. W.,'Unconscious Inference and Judgement in Perception', in J. M. Nicholas (ed.), *Images, Perception and Knowledge*, D. Reidel, Dordrecht, 1977, pp. 195–212.

HARTLEY, D., *Observations on Man*, 1749.

HAYEK, F. A., *The Sensory Order*, Routledge & Kegan Paul, London, 1952.

HEBB, D. O., *The Organization of Behavior*, Wiley, New York, 1949.

HIRST, P. H., *Knowledge and the Curriculum*, Routledge & Kegan Paul, London, 1975.

KANT, I., *The Critique of Pure Reason*, trans. N. Kemp Smith, Macmillan, London, 1929, rev. edn 1933 with reprints; St Martin's Press, New York, 1961.

KOHLER, W., *The Mentality of Apes*, Routledge & Kegan Paul, London, 1925.

MACKIE, J., 'Causes and Conditions', *American Journal of Philosophy*, vol. 2 (1965), pp. 245–64.

MISCHEL, T. (ed.), *Human Action: Conceptual and Empirical Issues*, Academic Press, New York, 1969.

MISCHEL, T. (ed.), *Cognitive Development and Epistemology*, Academic Press, New York, 1971.

MISCHEL, T. (ed.), *Understanding Other Persons*, Blackwell, Oxford, 1974.

PETERS, R. S., 'Moral Development and Moral Learning', *Monist*, 58 (1974), pp. 541–67.

PETERS, R. S., *Psychology and Ethical Development*, Allen & Unwin, London, 1974.

PETERS, R. S. (ed.), *The Concept of Education*, Routledge & Kegan Paul, London, 1967.

PETERS, R. S. (ed.), *The Philosophy of Education*, Oxford University Press, London, 1973.

PIAGET, J., *The Mechanisms of Perception*, Routledge & Kegan Paul, London, 1969.

PIAGET, J., *Biology and Knowledge*, Edinburgh University Press, 1971.

PIAGET, J., *Structuralism*, Routledge & Kegan Paul, London, 1971.

Bibliography

PIAGET, J., *The Principles of Genetic Epistemology*, Routledge & Kegan Paul, London, 1972.

PLATO, *Meno*.

PLATO, *Phaedo*.

PLATO, *Republic*.

PLATO, *Theaetetus*.

RAWLS, J., *A Theory of Justice*, Harvard University Press, 1971; Oxford University Press, London, 1972.

REID, T., *Essays on the Intellectual Powers of Man* (1785); ed. A. D. Woozley, Macmillan, London, 1941.

RUSSELL, B., *Logic and Knowledge*, ed. R. C. Marsh, Allen & Unwin, London, 1956.

RYLE, G., *The Concept of Mind*, Hutchinson, London, 1949.

SIBLEY, F. (ed.), *Perception*, Methuen, London, 1971.

SKINNER, B. F., *The Behavior of Organisms*, Appleton-Century-Crofts, New York, 1938.

SKINNER, B. F., *Verbal Behavior*, Appleton-Century-Crofts, New York, 1957.

STICH, S. P., 'What Every Speaker Knows', *Philosophical Review*, vol. 80 (1971), pp. 476–96.

TAYLOR, C., *The Explanation of Behaviour*, Routledge & Kegan Paul, London, 1964.

VENDLER, Z., *Res Cogitans*, Cornell University Press, Ithaca, NY and London, 1972.

WHITE, A. R., 'What We Believe', *Studies in the Philosophy of Mind, American Philosophical Quarterly*, monograph series No. 6 (1972), pp. 69–84.

WHITE, A. R. (ed.), *The Philosophy of Action*, Oxford University Press, London, 1968.

WITTGENSTEIN, L., *Philosophical Investigations*, Blackwell, Oxford, 1953.

WITTGENSTEIN, L., *On Certainty*, Blackwell, Oxford, 1969.

INDEX